The Spiritual Awakening:

Waking the Spiritually dead

&

Freeing the Spiritually Imprisoned

Jorrie Aja

Hurey-Scott

Table of Content

Chapter 1
How Much of What You do in Your Daily Living Do You Seek God About?

Matthew 6:30-34

30 Wherefore, if God so clothe the grass of the field, which today is, and tomorrow is cast into the oven, shall he not much more clothe you, O ye of little faith?

31 Therefore take no thought, saying, What shall we eat? or, What shall we drink? or, Wherewithal shall we be clothed?

32 (For after all these things do the Gentiles seek:) for your heavenly Father knoweth that ye have need of all these things.

33 But seek ye first the kingdom of God, and his righteousness; and all these things shall be added unto you.

34 Take therefore no thought for the morrow: for the morrow shall take thought for the things of itself. Sufficient unto the day is the evil thereof.

Romans 12:1-21

Jeremiah 29:11-13

11 For I know the thoughts that I think toward you, saith the Lord, thoughts of peace, and not of evil, to ive you an expected end.

12 Then shall ye call upon me, and ye shall o and pray unto me, and I will hearken unto you.

13 And ye shall seek me, and find me, when ye shall search for me with all your heart.

As a little spiritual foundation..... I went to a Catholic School from nursery school to 8th grade, then went to an all-girls Catholic High School all while being raised Presbyterian, but attended CME church every summer till I was about 14 years old.

So one thing I knew for sure is that there was, is, and always will be a God whom I trust and believe in with all my heart.

But who he was, and what he was capable of and His true role in life wasn't quite clear enough to live the life I now know I was created to live.

My true clarity came in 2006 when I personally decided to get to know for myself as an adult. Up until that moment what I had was Religion or I was religious, but I wanted more than the actions of Christian living. I wanted a relationship with my creator. The one who purposed and birthed me forward through my wonderful parents, whom I feel were specifically chosen to have me since I was the only time they had every gotten pregnant.

Shortly after I made this decision I became a member at a non-denominational church where I was introduced, blessed and baptized with the Holy Spirit, experienced a water baptism. There were several sudden changes, like my conscience which I now believe is the Holy Spirit leading and guiding me to live according to God's Word. The leading was strong and convicted me quicker when I was wrong or being sinful. Which initially was a little difficult cause I had to deny my fleshly desires, things that were normal(worldly), and some habitual.

At the start of this journey I decided it was time to read the Bible in its entirety. I knew a lot about the whole bible because of my upbringing. To learn for myself as an adult was something completely different. If you haven't, I urge you to, because depending on where you are in life reading the bible will mean something different. I have read versus at different times in my life and they mean something different; a friend can read the same versus and depending on where they are in life it could mean something different for them. The best part is... it all leads to the same end, you live and receive, according to God's instructions for life.

I didn't know if I should read it from front to back, back to front, inside out. Until I got some direction from God I would spot read(*pray to God to lead you to what he wants you to know, lay your Bible flat and open it and look down and the first thing your eyes focus on began to read).* The first time I opened to the Book of James, to me one of the shortest but powerful books in the Bible.

As I started at James 1:1-6 I was like wow joy/temptation, faith/patience, patience/perfect work, perfect and whole/wanting nothing, lack wisdom/ask God, faith/not wavering.

Initially I said to myself now that was straight to the point, Raw Truth!!!

Then it goes on to James 1:7-15 where it speaks of our mind, leading me to realize that the first thing to look at is our mindset. If you change your mind set you change your way of thinking and living. The verses start with what a man thinks, then the doubleminded man, men of low degree, the rich man, the blessed man, the tempted man, the lustful man and the consequences of these men.

This Book.... The Book of James speaks to all, it convicts you and advises of the rewards or promises you can expect.

Just when your mind thinks that you completely understand the truth... James tells of where things good and perfect come from, especially His truths.... The Word!

Who we are(a kind of first fruits of his creatures), how to hear(be swift to hear or listen), how to speak(slow to speak), and how to react(slow to wrath or anger). He quickly tells what wrath is not; It is not the righteousness of God.

He advises of how to act and what clearly isn't so good for our wellbeing (lay apart all filthiness and superfluity of naughtiness). He urges us to receive with meekness the engrafted Word, in order to save your soul.

I was in awe, I said God wants me to save myself first, so he can in turn use me to save others.

Just as that thought ended James 1:22 states "Be doers of the Word and not hearers only, deceiving your own selves".

I immediately asked God to show me, tell me, exactly how to act, behave, and live.

I realized at that moment The Holy Spirit showed me myself in that scripture. And Yes, I absolutely felt some kind a way. Then The Holy Spirit advised me that God corrects the ones he loves, but it only means something if I accept the correction and change it.

I was a hearer and reader of the word but my actions and daily living were not lining up. I began to think of all the things I knowingly do wrong that wouldn't please God and took steps day after day to change those things. And even now years later I still work on this. The fight is daily cause the devil works 365 days a year.

Then James 1:24 hit me with an image that wasn't quite favorable as my mind tried to process it. It tells us that those that only hear without doing is like a man holding his own face in a glass.

"He beholds himself and goes his own way and forgets the man he should be."

And then James gives life to laws of liberty...

"Those that continue and follow in those laws and be doers of the works that are just; This man shall be blessed in his deeds."

Bottom line follow the laws of freedom and do your part and you will be blessed.

In my mind it was received but I felt my spirit man beginning to process it. I immediately thought about laws literally that I may break but never get caught. As my mind began to think, I felt a prompting from the Holy Spirit.... Big or small; I immediately asked God to forgive me of those things. At that moment I moved forward with the mindset of following all laws. I have perfect driving record and I never thought it would make a big difference, but 6 years later I applied for a job that required me to have a clean driving record.

Remembering I gave a little of my spiritual background and what lead me to starting this journey...

I read on as the Book of James showed me my true self and how despite my so called religion and how I was raised believing in itself was enough and that *God knew my heart*. But then came James 1:26 "If any man among you seem to be religious and bridled not his tongue, but deceive his own heart, this man's religion is vain.

Again the word deceive seems to sting some, realizing that I had been half doing it, I was fooling myself thinking I had been doing enough. But the Holy Spirit kindly reminded me about grace and mercy which is what God has giving me so graciously. But there is something else if you choose to do it God's way you began to experience favor and supernatural blessings.

I remember thinking that God is so awesome that even as I lived sinfully he saw fit to bless me with grace and mercy and things were pretty good in the natural realm. Married, employed, one daughter at the time. But there were things I wanted that I couldn't quite understand why I wasn't getting it. I will get back to the wants of life.

I had to know more, I started to question why I had ignored these truths all these years and now that I know it, how much more is there and can I do it all. So…. On to James 2 more on God's expectation regarding our behavior/daily living.

James 2:2 advises us on the treatment of people(a man with a gold ring, in goodly apparel and there come in also a poor man in vile raiment) Rich vs Poor, the outward appearance as a manner of judging one another. In this verse the well-dressed or better off man appears to be respected and gave a better place to sit than the poor who was offered a footstool

My spirit man rejoiced finally something I didn't have to work on because I am almost opposite. I treat all people the same and will do for anyone. I have always been a giver and wanted to help people be better, live better, have better. But that too can be a dangerous thing because you tend to do it to a fault. Blocking God, instead of people going to God they go to willing givers.

After knowing I was hurting/enabling instead of actually helping I began to seek God before I do for others. God knows I am willing, but they too need to be willing to seek God first just as I have learned to do.

In James 2:5 we are told that God chose the poor of the world.... I blanked out for second and said it to myself "The poor people are poor cause God wants them to be.... But Why??

I read on "Hath not God chosen the poor of this world rich in faith, and heirs of the kingdom which he hath promised to them that love him?"

It reminds us that the world we live in despised the poor, it ask "is not the ones that oppress the poor rich, and places the lives of the poor out in the open for judgement.

God calls us to love our neighbor as thyself. We are all neighbors....

Then came a hard one James 2:9 "But if ye have respect to persons, ye commit sin and are convicted of the law as transgressors"

We can pick and choose between God's Laws and ignore others.....Ouch something I had been doing for years.

We have to act/behave expecting judgement based on God's laws of liberty(freedom)

Then James brings back faith in James 2:14 asking what does a man profit if he say he has faith but doesn't act as he does? Can faith save him? Back then I said yes, that answer changed!!!

Having faith, Real Faith in God's Word will manifest in your actions, behavior, and works. Having faith, being a doer of the work are Big Keys that you must carry and use. They are non-negotiable.

Then James 2:19 educated us on a truth you must really get:

> "Thou believe that there is one God; thou does well: the devils also believe and tremble."

As we all know Abraham believed God and had faith showed through his works.

James 2:26 summed it up "For as the body without the spirit is dead, so faith without works is dead also.

I felt this was boldly stated and no way to misinterpret it.

Chapter 2

How much of what you plan is based on what God has promised you, and all you can become?

In life there are a lot of things that go into shaping our lives and the direction we travel in.

We are greatly influenced by our parents and others we encounter in our early years. Think back to your earliest thoughts of what you wanted to be and what made you want to be that.

My first idea of what I wanted to be started out to be a teacher for kids with special need or disabled. Even at an early age I had compassion for people. At the age of 8 I realized computers and technology come easy to me, and some of the adults in my life began to sell the idea of technology and how it's the future. By the time I graduated from high school I had decided to major in computer information systems at ALL the colleges I attended and passed most classes with an A. It came easy to me much like mathematics.

Outside of these things I had some natural talents but no real focus was put on doing anything with those talents.

As an adult with children I have learned to pay attention to my children and what God has created them to be. Of course I want my children to be successful and healthy but more than that my biggest prayer for them is to be, and experience life as God intended. I don't want to be the reason my children's life is thrown off track.

I ask God to lead me in my role as a mother so that I plant fruitful seeds that they will reap a great harvest from.

As a parent, I can't selfishly impose my ideals on who my kids should be because I was only chosen to be a vessel to carry and birth my children. God is their creator and he chose them for a purpose just like me. It is God who will instruct the parents so that the end result is what God planned.

This is where we must realize and understand the importance of seeking God in all things, so that in all things you are in his will.

We can't be scared to dream, plan, and move forward in life. But if we connect to our creator and feed on the Word of God, we will dream and plan according to the word which will have us and our walk aligned with his Will.

His will is where we ALL belong and there is where we can and will experience the promises of God in all areas of our life.

James 3:1 "My brother, let not many of you become teachers knowing that we shall receive a stricter judgement."

This scripture made me look at myself and ask what am I teaching my children. Is my daily walk equipping them to walk as God instructed? Am I planting seeds of rebellion or obedience? Am I allowing God's truth to be exposed as I raise them and encourage them.

As I have seen through life parents that don't properly equip their children will pay a consequence later themselves.

Understanding God doesn't expect perfection, but your best. Remember God knows what your best looks like.

James 3:2-5

"We all stumble in many ways. Anyone who is never at fault in what they say is perfect, able to keep their whole body in check. When we put bits into the mouths of horses to make them obey us, we can turn the whole animal. Or take ships as an example. Although they are so large and are driven by strong winds, they are steered by a very small rudder wherever the pilot wants to go. Likewise, the tongue is a small part of the body, but it makes great boasts. Consider what a great forest is set on fire by a small spark"

Everyone stumbles and fails short, no one is perfect in all their ways. A perfect person is in control of all things, all the time, and only God has that character trait. We tend to think we are in control of more than we are. Only thing we control is our own right to choose, but the ability to follow through comes from God. You can't achieve alone what God planned.

God is the ultimate pilot and know where we are headed. In his will we can go through a storm and never get wet, dance in the fire and never get burned.

There is so much more to your life than you can see, be not deceived by what you see, but confidently trust God, His Word, and the Leading of the Holy Spirit.

Understanding the elements of who we are and what we are made of and the weapons God has given us to defeat the devil and his ways take away the fear of acting on the Word of God.

James 3:6-12

"The tongue also is a fire, a world of evil among the parts of the body. It corrupts the whole body, sets the whole course of one's life on fire, and is itself set on fire by hell. All kinds of animals, birds, reptiles and sea creatures are being tamed and have been tamed by mankind, but no human being can tame the tongue. It is a restless evil, full of deadly poison. With the tongue, we praise our Lord and Father, and with it we curse human beings, who have been made in God's likeness. Out of the same mouth come praise and cursing. My brothers and sisters, this should not be. Can both fresh water and salt water flow from the same spring? My brothers and sisters, can a fig tree bear an olive, or a grapevine bear a fig? Neither can a salt spring produce fresh water."

The tongue much like the other elements that make us who we are can and should be used for good, but anything can be misused and or used out of context. The tongue can be used to sow seed both of good and bad. Sometimes it will be your harvest to reap or the person's life in which you planted the seed, either way it's not guaranteed to be good just cause it was sown/planted.

What kind of fruit do you bear? It is true evidence of the seed others have sown in your life, and seed you had sown in your own life.

I tell people often that your life is evident of what you truly believe. You reap what you sow good or bad.

The more you act according to the word of God the less you will have to be concerned with the bad fruit, no matter if the seed was sown by you or someone else.

James 3:13-14

"Who is wise and understanding among you? Let them show it by their good life, by deeds done in the humility that comes from wisdom. But if you harbor bitter envy and selfish ambition in your hearts, do not boast about it or deny the truth."

This scripture tells us if we act, speak, and live according to the word which is truth, it makes God visible through our own willingness to speak and live his truth allowing our lives to be the evidence and our testimony.

James 3:15-16

"Such "wisdom" does not come down from heaven but is earthly, unspiritual, demonic. For where you have envy and selfish ambition, there you find disorder and every evil practice."

Be very careful of where you receive your knowledge and wisdom. Check for it in the Word of God for validation. Where God and his word is, there will be no confusion and no evil work.

James 3:17-18

"But the wisdom that comes from heaven is first of all pure; then peace-loving, considerate, submissive, full of mercy and good fruit, impartial and sincere. Peacemakers who sow in peace reap a harvest of righteousness."

Wisdom from heaven is pure and brings peace, is full of mercy and good fruits, and doesn't show favor or judge without correction.

Chapter 3

How much of what you want is based on what God Promises!

We all have wants, but like everything else we must analyze the driving force of our wants. Are they based on our parents? Our friends? Our Spouse? Or our kids?

At some point in my life I can say yes to each one of theses.

We will all come to point in our life where we have to understand God promises to meet our needs but when you are in the Will of God your desires and wants will be received as well. You will also realize that God created your dreams and desires as a way to provide direction and guidance.

Here is where I want to establish and make clear that we were created by God for a purpose and a plan. All through the bible God gives desires and dreams so we will have a undying fire and drive to get those things he has shown us. God gives us those things so we won't get distracted and thrown off course. To also ensure that his plan comes to pass!

Understanding who you are in Christ is Key. Without God there would be no you. You are because God is !!!

Our desires and dreams come from who God created us to be.

We also have to be careful about being to specific cause God can't be boxed in or contained.

Most times what we ask for is less than what God desires us to have.

For example, I use to pray for jobs and that's exactly what I would get. I had a desire and wanted to be employed and successful. God wants me to have a career not just a job.

Best thing I ever did was die to my own idea of what I believe God wanted me to be and do. I began to pray for God's will to be done in every area of my life. I believe in his vision, not because I know what it is. But because God created me to fulfill a specific purpose and he always has my best interest at heart. HIS vision became MY vision!!!!

Honestly it made my life easier and simpler, and ran into less issues and problems.

We tend to block God in our own effort. You don't know what's best for you over what God knows.

It's time to get in his Will and work on your purpose and his plan.

Which leads us to James 4!!!!

Before we start there you must base your wants and desires on the Word of God and not this world and today's society. And remember God won't require you to sacrifice who you were created to be for what he has planned and purposed you to be and have.

Your wants to should line up with the Word and God's Will for your life.

James 4:1

"What leads to strife (discord and feuds) and how do conflicts (quarrels and fighting) originate among you? Do they not arise from your sensual desires that are ever warring in your bodily members?"

Off the top James speaks of sensual desires and it's true that if those desires are at war in your body it will lead to strife and conflicts. I don't believe it's a coincidence that it's the 1st want covered.

James 4:2

"You are jealous and covet (what others have) and your desires go unfulfilled; So you become murderers (To hate is to murder as far as your heart is concerned). You burn with envy and anger and are not able to obtain (the ratification, he contentment and the happiness that you seek), so you fight and war. You do not have, because you do not ask."

We must learn that we were created as individuals and each for their own specific purpose and that purpose is yours to fulfill as you doing your part in the Kingdom of God.

What God has for you is for you and what God has destined you to have no man can take.

If we consider the statement you should never be jealous of who someone is or what they have because who they are and what they have was God's plan. Absolutely nothing was taken or withheld from you in order for God to give to them.

A hard lesson many have learned…. Chasing after someone else's dream will leave you lost and confused.

Truth is when you are on the right path and in the will of God, things flow smoothly and you can be certain of what your future holds.

The last part of James 4:2 "You do not have, because you do not ask"

This is not where you ask for what you want, but you ask for the things or wants that are based on the Word of God and all that he promises. This is how you receive YOUR promises.

I know you are thinking why do I have to ask. Asking God is one way God knows you have faith in him and his abilities and power. It also is your way of showing God you know you can't do it without him.

Even Jesus had 12 disciples.

Best thing you can do when you see others being blessed, rejoice and praise God for them and what they received.

When you are blessed to see od move in the lives of others, it is God's way of showing you what he can and will do for you.

God is no respector of persons what he will do for one he will do for another. But don't ask for what someone else has out of envy or jealousy, but because you believe in what God wants you to have and be.

James 4:3

"Do you ask God and yet fail to receive, because you ask with wrong purpose and evil, selfish motives. Your intention is to spend it in sensual pleasure."

Bottom line the purpose for which you ask HAS to be so you can become who God created you wo be, so you can fulfill your purpose in his plan.

Remember God doesn't fail.... We fail to change. We fail to believe. We fail to act as Gad says.

You can't check God, but you can check yourself!

James 4:4

"You are like unfaithful wives having illicit love affairs with the world and breaking your marriage vow to God! Do you not know that being the world's friend is being God's enemy? So whoever chooses to be a friend of the world takes his stand as an enemy of God."

This scripture speaks for itself. We are to live in this world but not be of this world.

Just like in Romans 12:1-3

"And so dear brothers and sisters, I plead with you to give your bodies to God because of all he has done for you. Let them be a living and holy sacrifice-the kind he will find acceptable. This is truly the way to worship him. Don't copy the behavior and customs of this world, but let God transform you into a new person by changing the way you think. Then you will learn to know God's will for you, which is good and pleasing and perfect. Because of the privilege and authority God has given me, I give each of you this warning: Don't think you are better than you really are. Be honest in your evaluation of yourselves measuring yourself by the faith God has given us."

See we are to live in the world and become who God created us to be despite the world and all its trouble and drama.

Only people affected by the world are worldly people.

In life I realize that it is absolutely true that we receive according to what we believe. Also your life is evidence of your beliefs. Our beliefs must be founded on the Word of God.

Romans: 12:5

"So it is with Christ's body, We are many parts of one body, and we all belong to each other."

Basically we all make up the Body of Christ but we all have our own purposes in achieving the overall plan.

Romans:12:6-8

"In his grace, God has given us different gifts for doing certain things well. So if God has given you the ability to prophesy, speak out with as much faith as God has given you. If your gift is serving others, serve them well. If you are a teacher, teach well. If your gift is to encourage others, be encouraging. If it is giving, give generously. If God has given you leadership ability, take the responsibility seriously. And if you have a gift for showing kindness to others, do it gladly."

Along with our purpose we also get gifts to use to do our part in the body of Christ. These are gifts from God not our parents or from going to school. James makes sure he informs us that not only are we to use our gifts for the Body of Christ but we do it with pleasure and joy.

James 4:5-6

"Do you doubt the Scriptures that say, "God truly cares about the Spirit he has put in us?" In fact God treats us with even greater kindness, just as the scripture say, "God opposes everyone who is proud, but he is proud, but he is kind to everyone who is humble."

James questions the belief of the reader and does it breed pride or lead to being humble as God instructed. You can be confident but not prideful. God blesses the humble.

James 4:7

"Surrender to God! Resist the devil and he will run from you. Come near to God, and he will come near to you. Clean up your lives, you sinners. Purify your hearts you people who can't make up your mind"

Surrender….. Resist….. Watch the devil flee. Once the devil does flee James instructs us to come near to God and he will come to you. Do your part and with faith and certainty God will do his part.

When James says clean up your lives he wants us to learn God's truth and obey his Word and change according to the Word of God. Purifying your heart would be you having the heart of Jesus, as well as the inability to make up our minds, leads us to why we should have the mind of Christ.

James 4:10

"Be humble in the Lord's presence, and he will honor you."

Being humble means being free from pride or thinking more of ones self than you should. To be comfortable with who you are in Christ.

James 4:11-12 advises us about saying cruel things about others!

"My friends, don't say cruel things about others! If you do, or if you condemn others, you are condemning God's law. And if you condemn the Law, you put yourself above the law and refuse to obey either it or God who gave it. God is our judge and he can save or destroy us. What right do you have to condemn anyone."

The devil condemns us!

God convicts us.

Condemning is about tearing a person down, making them feel shame.

John12:47 "I am not the one who will judge those who refuse to obey my teachings. I came to save the people of this world, not be their judge."

Romans 8:1-2 "If you belong to Christ Jesus, you won't be punished. The Holy Spirit will give you life that comes from Christ Jesus and will set you free from sin and death."

Conviction is also known as Godly sorrows. God convicts us of our wrongs, meaning he shows us our wrong but corrects or gives a solution. This should lead us to repentance and God's forgiveness.

James 4:13-16 warns us about bragging and the pitfalls there of.

"You should know better than to say, "Today or tomorrow we will go to the city. We will do business there for a year and make a lot of money. What do you know about tomorrow? How can you be so sure about your life? It is nothing more than mist that only appears for only a little while before it disappears. You should say "If the Lord lets us live, we will do these things. Yet you boast in your presumptions and your self-conceit. All such boast is wrong."

This is simple and easy to understand. No bragging or boasting, but we can acknowledge who we are in Christ.

This life isn't about us, but about who God created us to be, see, experience, and achieve.

But all the Glory belongs to Him!

James ends chapter 4 with raw truth

James 4:17

"So any person who knows what is right to do but does no do it, that in itself is sin.

Once you know the truth about what you are doing, it becomes sin to continue on in that thing.

This is where the lies and deceit keep you bound to negative strongholds that keep you separated from God.

Accept the fact that you don't know all the rights and wrongs.

But as you experience life God convicts and corrects us at that time it is up to us to practice doing what is right. You will fail sometimes but we are to keep going in our efforts to do what is right in God's eyes.

God promises us a lot to in our life time. In order to receive we must practice obedience to God and his world. We must live and operate in the will of God to receive according to the Word.

More often than not we know the promise but ignore the words that lead us to that promise. We can believe, but receiving takes us to act.

Believe according to the Word!

Act according to the Word!

Receive according to the Word!

Once you know the truths of God and the Word and you began to have the mind of Christ you will being to only want what God has for you and promised. You will began to pray according to his Word and receive according to the Word.

Chapter 4

How much of what you think you need is based on what God promises to provide?

Because we are human there are a lot of things that play a part in our thoughts. Experiences, environment, and the individuals you have encountered thus far.

Truth is we are supposed to have the mind of Christ and think as Jesus thinks and believes.

1 Corinthians 2:16

"For who hath know the mind of the Lord that he may instruct him? But we have the mind of Christ"

Romans 12:2

"And be not conformed to this world: but be ye transformed by the renewing of your mind, that ye may prove what is good and acceptable and perfect will of God."

1 Corinthians 2:13-16

"And we are setting these truths forth in words not taught by human wisdom but taught by the Holy Spirit, combining and interpreting spiritual truths with spiritual language. But the natural nonspiritual man received not the things of the spirit of God: for they are foolishness unto him: neither can he know them, because they are spiritually discerned."

Philippians 2:5

"Let this mind be in you, which was also is Christ Jesus"

John 5:3-4

"In this day a great multitude of sick people – some blind, some cripple, some paralyzed – waiting for the bubbling up of the water. For an angel of the Lord went down at appointed seasons into the pool and moved and stirred up of the water, stepped in and was cured of whatever disease with which he was afflicted."

This chapter brings in to perspective of needs over wants. We often get the two confused or mixed up.

Our needs cover the things obtained to sustain us mentally and physically. These are the things God promises us.

Our wants have more to do with our flesh and world desires. When we operate from a place of flesh it is because we are being of the world not just in. We are supposed to live on earth in the natural realm, but reside and operate in the supernatural.

In life we act according to the Word of God we receive according to that same Word. But we act according to this world you will reap worldly consequences.

I was raised believing things go a certain way for all people if they follow the same path. That is not the case and can cause you to drift or go off course from the plan of God for your life.

We must start early understanding God and the fact that he saw our ending and then created us to be born. Most people get off track early because the ones leading and guiding us are not being led by God or the Holy Spirit.

In my journey, this process taught me that the mindset must change and your thought process should operate with the Word of God being the standard or set guideline and foundation.

There are a lot of ways to get your mind under the Authority of God and his Word.

1) First way is to research biblically who God is and his role, his plan, his purpose and how he work. This can take you by storm because God is all powerful, All knowing, the Alpha and the Omega and so much more. Next would be to find out who, and what God says about you which often times contradicts what society, friends, and family think or believe about you. The last thing would be to research Jesus' journey from beginning to end, which leads you to doing the research about the Holy Spirit.

2) Go to church (A church that feeds you spiritually). Attend bible study and join some ministries, within your church home.

3) Develop a healthy prayer and meditation Life.

4) Feed your spirit man daily, giving God time with you every day. This feeding can come from Christian music, prayer, meditation, fasting, read/studying the Word of God, read books by people who you connect and can relate and receive from spiritually.

You must have a starting point and a plan, so time and energy are not wasted. You may look at these things and feel you don't have enough time. You must make time for God and the building of that relationship.

What I realize more now than ever, I wasted a lot of time doing thing that were irrelevant and had or served any purpose. Instead I realize that the devil does come to steal, kill, and destroy and of his more important tools were distractions and deception.

The devil has a way of distracting us with things, ideas, and situations that feed the flesh only or sows unfruitful seed in our own life as well as those around us.

What we think directly impacts what we believe which in turn affects what we receive. Which is one reason why it is important to have the mind of Christ. Having the mind Christ opens out mind to unimaginable and the unobtainable according to our flesh.

Once we truly believe something, we can than expect t receive according to the Word. Expecting God to do exactly as his Word says speaks to our faith not our arrogance.

I expect with a certainty for I know God is not a man and he cannot lie.

Our thoughts must be ...... need to be...... according to the Word of God. The Word of God holds such power and authority. But it gives us instruction, guidance, hope, and parable that shows us that God is the same today, yesterday and forever more.

I went through a season where God exposed everyone in my life and what they really think of me. I call this a people inventory check. God also showed me the purpose of me in their life and them in mine. I can tell you today it changed my circle drastically and I am very conscious as to who I allow in. If you are honest with yourself when you ask why is this person in my life, what purpose does it serve, and does it help me become who God created you to be.

Relationship Inventory

- Start with your everyday people. This can include parents, best friends, etc.
- Co-Workers and people your speak with monthly, Bi-yearly, or even yearly
- Questions:
    - What is the purpose of the relationships and whom does it serve?
    - Does the person withdraw from you without making any deposits(Everyone isn't suppose to make deposits)?

- Do they have a working relationship with God? Do they value your relationship w/ God more than they value their own relationship with God?
- How does this relationship help you fulfill your purpose?
- How does this relationship help in the process of becoming who God created you to be?

After you complete the inventory you will have some decisions/choices to make about how you deal with people and how you affect people you have relationships with.

Also notice that relationships do change because we grow or don't grow at different rates. So who one person is today this time next year their purpose in your life can and will change.

Once you get your mind/thought life under God's Word, what your do, how you react, how you respond will all change. And this will directly affect your life experience and how you experience life. It will also change both your perception and perspective.

Some people, things, issues, and circumstance as God does is life changing!
.......FOR THE BETTER!!!!!!

The wants will eventually be based on what God promises, because you have the mind of Christ. Funny part is once you find out all God has promised you realize with the old wants you were shorting yourself in more ways than one.

Chapter 5
The Spiritual Awakening

The spiritual awakening is a process within the process of becoming who God created you to be.

Initially in this process the Word of God is alive and working in your life. You see the Word of God as a complete truth. A truth that all things for you stem from the Word of God. The Word of God will be your primary guide, no other truth will rise above the truth that flows from the Word of God.

Psalm 119:105

"Thy Word is a lamp unto my feet and light unto my path."

John 14:6

"Jesus saith unto him, I am the way, the truth, and the life: no man cometh unto the Father but by me.

John 17:17

"Sanctify them through thy truth: thy Word is truth.

The more we are led by the truth, God's Word, the less we fall for the tricks and deception of Satan.

One of the 1st truths is that there is a spiritual war going one.

Seeing things as God does

Seeing things as God does will change the game, it will change your day to day living, your perception of the things you will encounter, and all you can do and achieve.

God makes it plain in the bible. The bible is a guide on living, all areas ae addressed. There are no new things that will ever arise that the Bible cant help you understand or get clarity.

In todays world we are greatly impacted by the worldly, social media, reality shows(fake), the media. We are letting the world set standards, where God has already done so. This only throws us off and out of the Will of God. We are not to conform to this world. You cant do what the world requires to achieve and fulfill your purpose. Your actions, behaviors and decisions should be aligned with the Word of God so that you receive according to the Word, experience according to the Word; Becoming who God created you to be and do all you were put here to be and all you were created to impact.

Romans 12:2

"Don't conform to this world, but be transformed by the renewal of your mind, that by testing you may discern what is the Will of God, what is good and acceptable and perfect"

Philippians 4:8

"Finally, Brothers whatever is true, whatever is honorable, whatever is just, whatever is pure, whatever is lovely, whatever is commendable, if there is any excellence, if there is anything worthy of praise, think about these things"

Isaiah 26:3

"You keep him in perfect peace whose mind is stayed on you, because he trust in you"

2 Corinthians 10:3-6

"We are human, but we don't wage war as humans do. We use God's mighty weapons, not worldly weapons, to knock down the strongholds of human reasoning and to destroy false arguments. We destroy every proud obstacle that keeps people from knowing God. We capture their rebellious thoughts and teach them to obey Christ. And after you have become fully obedient, we will punish everyone who remains disobedient."

James 1:8

"Their Loyalty is divided between God and the world, and they are unstable in everything they do."

Ephesians 4:22-24

"throw off your old sinful nature and your former way of life, which is corrupted by lust and deception. Instead, let the spirit renew your thoughts and attitudes. Put on your new nature, created to be like God-truly righteous and holy.

Proverbs 4:23

"Above all else, guard your heart for everything you do flows from it"

2 Corinthians 5:17

"This means that anyone who belongs to Christ has become a new person. The old life is gone; a new life has begun!"

Once we accept God as our creator and believe that Jesus died on the cross for our sin. The Word of God becomes truth and an ever-guiding life to us being a new creature in Christ.

We now get to wake up daily, choosing God his way and his Word. When doing this you will have a certain confidence in who you are and the intent of all you do.

God's way is without burden and doubt, a life of certainty without confusion.

It's a fact you were uniquely made to do only what you can do. No one will do what you were created to do. True, the path and journey there isn't always favorable, but God is not wasteful and it's always a lesson to take from every life encounter and life experience.

It is also true that chasing what the world is offering will not lead you to your purpose, you must seek God and his Word to get that.

You have to learn about who God says you are, and you will see how wrong the world is about you and all you can do.

This world is all about labels, limits, an standards based on what it offers and can contain. The only label you need to wear is "A child of God". "A child of the Great I am." The labels the world gives us is so they can divide, categorize, control and contain who we become what we can have, and what we experience all of which is against what God says and wants for us.

We must recognize the source of all things, its either God or the devil. There is no gray area. The gray area only exists for those who straddle the fence saying the know God exist and he is real BUT live according to the world expecting to receive what God promises. Conforming to this world will allow you to reap from this world. Pray, study the Word, live according to the Word, believe the Word, and receive according to the Word.

God is very specific about not conforming. During my studying of the topic there are at least 34 scriptures that speak on conforming: (remember knowing the truth allows you to operate freely in worldly realm and the supernatural realm)

- Romans 12:2
- 1 Peter 1:14
- Exodus:23:2
- Leviticus: 20:23

- Deuteronomy 18:9
- 2 Kings 17:15
- Ezekiel 11:12
- Daniel 1:8
- Ephesians 4:17
- Colossians 3:7-8
- 1 Thessalonians 5:6
- 1 timothy 1:9-11
- 1 Peter 4:3
- Romans 8:29
- John 13:15
- Romans 13:14
- 1 Corinthians 11:1
- Ephesians 5:1-2
- Philippians 2:5
- Romans 6:3-10
- 2 Corinthians 4:10
- Romans 8:10-11
- Philippians 3:10-11
- 1 Peter 4:13
- Philippians 3:10
- Galatians 6:14
- Colossians 1:24
- Colossians 3:3
- 1 Peter 2:21
- 1 Peter 4:1
- Ephesians 2:4-6

- 1 Corinthians 15:20-22
- Colossians 3:1

Freedom to act according to the Word

True freedom is when one can openly and willingly do what God tells them without any hinderance.

To do this you must believe always, that God has your best interest at heart so in this part of your process you will trust God no matter what you see. In this part of your process you must challenge every though and action to recognize the source.

There are only 2 sources in which our thought flow from, its either God or the devil. There is no gray area. The gray area only exists for those that want to reside in the natural realm, or they reside in the spiritual realm but desire the things of this world.

Choose a side, your journey can't truly begin until you pick a side and operate in that realm.

If you choose to reside in the Spirit realm, that is where supernatural blessing and favor will be received. In the Spirit realm is where you reside and experience the promises of God. It is the realm where the Word of God holds the most power. Where you obey and live a doubtless life confidently moving forward with expectation in your heart.

If you choose to reside in the worldly realm that is where God gives us freely grace and mercy is received. But if you reside and conform to this world you can expect to receive according to what the world offers. Which is nothing compared to the spirit realm.

When recognizing the source of all things you will question if the outcome of the thought or action will push you closer to God, your purpose, and his plan for yourself. If it pulls you away, distract, deter you away from God, the Word, your purpose, his plan....

Stop and give that thought!

The devil has never changed his plan, his goal is to kill, steal, and destroy us from becoming all God created us to be and HE WILL NEVER STOP.

We must be aware of who the devil is and how he operates, just the same as if we want to know who we are, we must know who our creator is.

In my research and studying on this topic I was led to a book called "Outwitting the Devil" By Napoleon Hill. This book had 12 chapters and it was basically an interview with the devil. After reading it my eyes were wide open, and I was aware of the devil, his presence, how he functioned, and ALL his tools. I felt stronger in my walk and was able to take confident steps in my journey.

In this book the devil was asked where he lived and describe his physical appearance?

The Devil responded by saying he has no physical body. He also states he consist of negative energy and lives in the minds of people who fear him. He also stated he occupies one-half of every atom of physical matter and every unit of mental and physical energy. He simply stated he is the negative portion of the atom.

At some point the devil explained how he controls the minds of 98 out of every 100 people. He stated that he gains control of the minds of people by merely moving in and occupying the unused space of the human brain. He stated he sows the seed of negative thought in the minds of people so he can occupy and control the space.

The devil stated that one of his cleverest devices for mind control is fear. He plants seeds of fear in the minds of people, and as these seeds germinate and grow, through use, he then controls the space they occupy.

The devil claimed the 6 most effective fears are:

1) Fear of poverty
2) Criticism
3) Ill Health
4) Loss of love
5) Old Age
6) Death

He also claims 1 and 6 are the fears that serve him the most.

But this is just a little of what I read. I would encourage you to read it for yourself and draw your own conclusions.

But you can't defeat what you don't understand!

After reading, researching, studying, and meditating, I understand that our thoughts stem from and feed2 off the thought seeds planted by God or the devil. Depending on your choices, beliefs, and where you choose to operate from those seeds will manifest and grow and ultimately help guide your life, experiences, day to day living, and our future.

We must learn to recognize the source of all things. Don't be afraid to challenge your own thoughts, actions, and behaviors against the Word of God. Ask yourself does this thought, action, words, response pull me closer to God, help me on my journey as I go through my process or does it distract me, deter me, pull me away from God and where he has taken me from and leading me too!

Once you gain the understanding of who you are according to God, we will learn about the authorities we have, but rarely use. Often we go through life not actively participating in our journey and process.

Life truly begins when you choose God's will with all your heart and live according to the Word of God and receive according to the Word.

The Word of God is like the 1st breath breathed into Adam.

God loves us so much! He gave us an instruction guide, and a Savior. We must recognize how blessed we are. The Bible is universal, and the rules and regulations apply the same to everyone equally across the board.

The standards have been set, don't conform to the world. God gave us all the same rules but created us to be different and uniquely made while setting the path that will lead us to a God appointed end.

Remember Jesus was Jesus at birth, even before birth. God knew his ending before he was formed in his mother's womb. This is the same for us. He saw who we would become before he formed us and put us in our mother's womb.

For this to hold true, we must acknowledge that everything is connected. God isn't wasteful, but he is very intentional.

Who you are to become is more about who created you to be than how you entered this earth.

If we consider how Jesus was created and the state in which his family lived and the unfavorable conditions, tells us that how we enter this world and our environment in which we were raised doesn't determine our purpose. How Jesus was birthed and the early hard times his family encountered had no bearing on his future. But God still has never been surprised or caught off guard by the things we do, say, or what someone may do or say to us.

But this is where we trust God no matter what. In order to trust in the manner, you must read your Bible and understand who God is, how he speaks, how he operates. Then you will know what to listen for and look out for. How can you know yourself when don't know the one who created you? How can you be prepared if you aren't aware of the devil, and how he operates?

Read your bible and study your bible. Make your relationship with God a priority.

I challenge you to read "Outwitting the Devil" By Napoleon Hill and form your own opinion. I guarantee either way your eyes will be wide open, and you will have clarity about God, the devil and yourself.

Chapter 6 The Devil's Ploy: game Changes when the Awakening Begin

The World's View

Deceive – (of a person) cause (someone) to believe something that is not true, typically in order to gain some personal advantage.

> ➤ Give a mistaken impression

> ➤ Fail to admit to oneself that something is true

> ➤ Be sexually unfaithful(one's regular partner)

Deceives – (3rd person present), Deceived (past tense),

Deceived – (past participle), Deceiving (present participle)

Additional definition

- To cause to believe what is not true; mislead

- To catch by guile; ensnare

Act of being deceitful – To practice deceit

                              To give a false impression

This world's view of you is distorted and only created to confine, label, control, mislead, and deceive us.

The Bible already told us who we are and God's plan for us. Anything that contradicts the Word of God should be disregarded. Don't allow the idea or thought to enter your mind or spirit.

The world's view of you, what you can achieve, and the best way to live; will lead you astray. The world's view will cause you to live in doubt, fear and uncertainty. When God so graciously gave us his son to save us, the Holy Spirit to guide us, and the Word of God to instruct us. The world's version of help or guidance only leads us further from the truth; that God intended us to be set free by!

The world puts forth a lot of effort to label any and all people so they can be categorized and set the standard of behavior where life outcomes are predicted and even advised as to what everyone can expect.

But God.....

Created us to all be unique in every way, each with their own identity and created for a specific purpose. God has called you to do something only you can do. That thought in itself contradicts the world and its view, because the world wants us to be the same, strive for the same goals/American dream.

The only reason people desire the same as someone else is because they believe what the world says good, and what is best.

The world and its views are filled with limited, and fake standards that only prevent us from fulfilling our full potential, living out our destiny, and doing things that have never been done.

Our instructions for life are the same but because God made us uniquely different, the outcomes will all be different but serve a great purpose in the Kingdom of God.

God wants us to reach beyond the limits of this world. He exist beyond the worldly limits.

Once you accept the labels this world has created, you began to follow the structure this world sets to confine you so they can predict your future while calling you a statistic.

Refuse to be labeled anything other than a Child of God. That label should describe your behavior.

Child of God - The Label

Behavior - Christlike

Thought Life - Have the mind of Christ

Morals/Value - Set by the Word. Pay attention to the changes from the old to the New Testement

Future - Nothing is impossible with God

Health - 1 Peter 2:24 "He himself bore our sins in his body on the tree, that we mighmight die to sin and live righteousness. By his wounds you have been healed.

Most of what this world is selling is less than what God is offering. God gave us the freedom to choose.

The world wants to control us so they can keep us nound to the things God himself said we would overcome and conquer.

This is where the true knowledge of God will free us to be all that he says and more than this world could handle. Be bold in your walk, know in your heart, mind, body, and spirit what it means if you belong to God and you believe that his son died on the cross for our sins and transgressions.

We are already saved, but we listen to this world as they tell us that they are saving us or helping us. We freely give away our power by not believing and operating according to the Word of God.

This world misleads and deceives us by defining success, beauty, wealth, education requirements and even as fas as defining what is considered a "Good Life", a good education, a good job, and a good marriage.

Do not be deceived, no two people are a like nor will their life choices or outcomes be remotely similar.

Value the differences between you and you and your spiritual brothers and sisters.

When trying to understand how things go wrong, we must consider there are over 100 scriptures that speak on deception.

In order to avoid being deceived, mislead or thrown of course; here I will give you scriptural foundation on deception which is one of the devils most used weapons. His very 1st trick was deceiving Eve despite her knowing God's truth. Sounds familiar!!!!! Exactly..............

True freedom is found in the Word of God.

The Truth Based on Scripture from the Old Testament

There is such freedom in knowing and living according to the Word of God also known as the Bible. The more you know, it allows you to operate and live according to the Word. Unfortunately, the world is so tainted the bible often times contradicts the world and its belief system. Which has tripped people up for years and generations.

There are a lot of scriptures and Bible stories that involve deception. I pulled over 100 scriptures from 30 different chapters; 9 from the Old Testament and 21 from the New Testament.

Genesis

3:4 "then the Serpent said to the woman, you will not surely die."

God was specific in his instructions and the conscience and Satan did the exact same thing but spoke contradictory to God's Words. The Serpent even went as far as to tell you the benefits (So called) to disobeying God. I don't believe God ever intended for us to know both good and evil. Like any other good thing the devil will find a way to distort and pervert it.

Exodus

20:16 "You must not testify falsely against your neighbor."

Bottom line don't lie or speak false information regarding other. This can also be considered you sowing bad seed.

Deuteronomy

11:16 "Beware that your hearts are not deceived and that you do not turn away from the Lord and serve other gods and worship them."

This scripture is one reason God tells us to guard our hearts and minds.

In order to protect your heart and not be deceived we can not operate from a place controlled by our emotions.

Emotions are mistakenly associated with compassion. Emotion is defined as a natural instinctive state of **_MIND_** deriving from one's circumstances, mood, or relationship with others. A second definition is an instinctive or intuitive feeling as distinguished from reasoning or knowledge.

Emotions are often irrational and will send you off because they serve your flesh and will cause you to act out of character and do things that would not please God or get you the results your heart and mind desire.

What happens after our hearts are deceived, unfortunately we often times blame God for the bad behavior of others causing us to turn from him and his ways. Giving value to a false sense of love designed to cater to our flesh and causing us to act inappropriately and value what soothes the ache no matter the moral standard of behavior.

25:13-16(nlt) " You must use accurate scales when you weigh out merchandise, and you must use full and honest measures. Yes, always use honest weights and measures, so that you may enjoy a long life in the land of the Lord your God is giving you. All who cheat with dishonest weights and measures are detestable to the Lord your God.

25:13-16(esv) " You shall not have in your bag 2 kinds of weights, a large, and a small. You shall not have in your house 2 kinds of measure, a large and a small. A full and fair weight you shall have, a full and fair measure you shall have, that your days may be long in the land that the Lord your God is giving you. For all who do such things, all who act dishonestly, are an abomination to the Lord your God."

I thought it would be good to show these two versions of the same scripture. The 1st one speaks in terms of Good/products/merchandise in terms of how they are valued and distributed and the standard set to determine should be based of the fullness of the product and the honest use and necessity of the goods. Based on this scripture being fair and keeping within honest standards you shall live long in the land/place God has provided for you.

The 2nd version speaks to allowing one measure or standard to govern your home and the measure or weight should not change, it should be the same for all establishing what is honest and fair. When one is honest and fair, God can trust you with his promise because he is certain that we will do and give according to his Word and his Will.

God wants things to be based on a full and fair measure not based on color, status, looks, etc.

Judges

16:4-20 "Judges 16:4-20 Amplified Bible (AMP)

After this he fell in love with a Philistine woman living in the Valley of Sorek, whose name was Delilah. So the five lords governors of the Philistines came to her and said to her, "Persuade him, and see where his great strength lies and find out how we may overpower him so that we may bind him to subdue him. And each of us will give you eleven hundred pieces of silver." So Delilah said to Samson, "Please tell me where your great strength lies and with what you may be bound and subdued." Samson said to her, "If they bind me with seven fresh cords tendons that have not been dried, then I will be weak and be like any [other] man." Then the Philistine lords brought her seven fresh cords that had not been dried, and she bound him with them. Now she had men lying in ambush in an inner room. And she said to him, "The Philistines are upon you, Samson!" And he broke the cords as a string of tow breaks when it touches fire. So the secret of his strength was not discovered. Then Delilah said to Samson, "See now, you have mocked me and told me lies; now please tell me truthfully how you may be bound." He said to her, "If they bind me tightly with new ropes that have not been used, then I will become weak and be like any other man." So Delilah took new ropes and bound him with them and said to him, "The Philistines are upon you, Samson!" And the men lying in ambush were in the inner room. But he snapped the ropes off his arms like sewing thread. Then Delilah said to Samson, "Until now you have mocked me and told me lies; tell me truthfully] with what you may be bound." And he said to her, "If you weave the seven braids of my hair with the web and fasten it with a pin, then I will become weak and be like any other man." So while he slept, Delilah took the seven locks/braids of his hair and wove them into the web. And she fastened it with the pin of the loom and said to him, "The Philistines are upon you, Samson!" And he awoke from his sleep and pulled out the pin of the weaver's loom and the web. Then she said to him, "How can you say, 'I love you,' when your heart is not with me? You have mocked me these three times and have not told me where your great strength lies." When she pressured him day after day with her words and pleaded with him, he was annoyed to death. Then finally he told her everything that was in his heart and said to her, "A razor has never been used on my head, for I have been a Nazirite to God from my mother's womb. If I am shaved, then my strength will leave me, and I will become weak and be like any other man." Then Delilah realized that he had told her everything in his heart, so she sent and called for the Philistine lords, saying, "Come up this once, because he has told me everything in his heart." Then the Philistine lords came up to her and brought the money they had promised in their hands. [19] She made Samson sleep on her knees, and she called a man and had him shave off the seven braids of his head. Then she began to abuse Samson, and his strength left him. She said, "The Philistines are upon you, Samson!" And he awoke from his sleep and said, "I will go out as I have time after time and shake myself free." For Samson did not know that the LORD had departed from him.

This scripture brings to light emotions and being misled despite knowing better. Sampson retaliated against the Philistines because of the wife swap. These actions on behalf of both parties lead to vengeful efforts. Because Sampson loved Delilah, it was easy for him to overlook her deception and even gave into her request to know how to weaken him. Deceit only leads to more deceit and broken trust, which can lead to individuals having trust issues with God and others.

<u>1 Kings</u>

13:18(the disobedient prophet) "He answered him, "I too am a prophet, as you are; and an angel spoke to me by the word of the Lord, saying "Bring him back with you to your house , so that he may eat bread and drink water." But he lied to him.""

This scripture covers deceit of another kind, one we all face and encounter. Very much like what Adam and Eve had to face. God gave the man of God direct instructions on what not to do and where not to go. The old prophet lied about what God told him, and disobey God's original instructions. God gives us all instruction and orders our steps. God isn't a God of confusion. He would never instruct us one way and send us another with instructions to directly contradict what God said. The devil is slick in that way. His goal is to always disprove God, his will, his way, and his Word. Don't help the devil devalue what God gave you. In God's instructions and guidance there is protection and assurance of what is to come according to God's plan.

Psalms

24:3-5 "Who may ascend onto the mountains of the Lord? And who may stand in His Holy place? He who has clean hands and a pure heart. Who has not lifted up his soul to what is false, nor has sworn deceitfully(never tell lies), they will receive the Lord's blessings and have a right relationship with God their savior."

I love Psalms and how God uses scripture to teach, guide, instruct, warn, urge, and correct us. This scripture tells us what it takes to ascend to be closer to God and who can stand in his Holy Presence and Holy Place. Your hands must be clean, meaning free of wrong doing; your heart must be pure, meaning a heart for God, his ways, and his Word. This person must also be loyal and have faith in God and God alone. No one or no thing should be placed ahead of God. The reward far exceeds what is required. For these things will bring about you receiving a blessing for the Lord and righteousness from the God of his salvation.

Obedience to God will do more for you than following others and their rules.

37:8-9 "Stop being angry! Turn from your rage! Do not lose your temper, it only leads to harm for the wicked will be destroyed, but those who trust in the Lord will possess the Land.

This scripture was very specific leaving little room for misinterpretation. This scripture is also speaking yet again on emotions and how to not allow them to control you or the consequences, and reward giving a fair depiction of how God feels about anger, which causes one to rage, losing your temper causing you to act inappropriately or to do things you cannot take back. Often times sowing a bad seed that you will one day reap. God warns us of what lies ahead for the wicked, and what is to come for those that trust him.

52:2 "Your tongue plots destruction, like a sharp razor, you are a worker of deceit."

This scripture put into perspective that your behavior dictates your intent. This scripture continues to show how our words or our tongue can be used as a mighty weapon as destruction for us as individuals or others. The clear message here is if the intent of your words or tongue is to destroy, it defines you as a deceiver.

101:7 "I will not allow deceivers to serve in my house and liars will not stay in my presence."

Good Word right here!!!!!!

Once the deceivers have been identified, understand that if that is who they are they aren't allowed to serve in God's house, big chance of bad seeds being sown corrupting others in the house or even the peace and foundation the house rest on. God goes on to specify which type deceiver can or can't be in he or stay in his presence if they are liars.

Lies serve no purpose but to deceive, and sow bad seeds. There levels to deception, being a liar or lying is just one form.

The truth will always lead to freedom. There is never a good time or a reason to lie.

Lying will always be used as way to deceive!!!

Stop lying, speaking the truth will allow and give God the opportunity to use you to speak the truth.

Practice speaking only the truth. Don't be swayed by your feelings and emotions.

Telling yourself the truth will help you not believe the lies from others.

Proverbs

10:9(amp) "He who walks in integrity and with moral character walks securely, But he who takes a crooked way will be discovered and punished.

10:9(nlt) "People with integrity walk safely, but those who follow crooked paths will exposed.

For this scripture, both translations seem necessary to make the point clear. First let's define integrity. Integrity is the quality of being honest and having strong moral principles, moral uprightness. Integrity can also be the state of being whole and undivided. When I think of integrity, I think of the intent behind the behavior or actions is key. Being honest and living morally according to the Word of God helps lead us to having integrity in all that we do or say. Being and living a life of integrity ensures protection and safety.

The scripture boldly says what happens when you choose the wrong path or road or make the wrong conscious choice, you will be discovered, punished, and exposed. How dare we not take heed! Recollect how many times you chose wrong for the wrong reason, chose a path that was not in line with God's Will for your life and ended up exposed and portrayed improperly, and punished unfairly.

This is an instance where listening to the Holy Spirit or your conscience, and having safe, true and Godly intentions.

11:3 "Honesty guides good people; dishonesty destroys treacherous people."

This scripture is both clear and understandable. Honesty is a place we should all operate from, to protect and control the outcome. Honesty leads to an expected end. Honest people or people lead by the intent of being honest is a great thing to have in your life and your circle. Being around and in the company of honest people will help you lead a honest life. Being dishonest is bad for all parties involved whether you are the one being dishonest or someone else is being dishonest with you. It is bad seed sown on both sides. Being dishonest makes you untrustworthy which taints the view in which one sees another. There is never a good reason to be dishonest and it speaks to ones character.

12:22(amp) "Lying lips are extremely disgusting to the Lord, But those who deal faithfully are his delight."

12:22(nlt) "The Lord detest lying lips, but he delights in those who tell the truth."

Both translations seem necessary to truly show how God really feels about lying and those that lie. God feels strongly because he knows that when someone lies they are working with Satan whether they know it or not. The devil uses anyone willing to do his dirt and play a part in his overall and ultimate goal to kill, steal, and destroy as well as disprove God, his Power, his Word, and his Will.

Beware do not allow the devil to use you or your lips to lie or be dishonest. Never try and justify a lie or dishonesty, it will only lead to more deception, lies, and dishonesty.

Lies are tools of the devil and they manifest as bad seeds sown.

15:1 "A soft, gentle, and thoughtful answer turns away the wrath, but harsh, painful, and careless words stir up anger.

In this scripture the descriotive words used are key. Being soft in tone, gentle in spirit, and thoughtful speaking to the consciousness of the circumstance, and controlling your response based on who God is and who he created you to be instead of letting other elements control your approach or response. Don't be swayed by the incorrect behavior of others.... Stay Focus!!! God's Word stands true.

Being harsh in tone, causing painful encounters, being careless are all used to stir up our spirit and improperly engage our flesh with the intent of making it rise, causing one to act out of your true character. Recognize the devil's work trying to disrupt your spirit and cause you to do what is not pleasing to God.

19:1 "Better to be poor and honest than to be rich, dishonest, and a fool."

I'm sure we all look at the scripture regarding the poor and always feel such compassion in our hearts.

Being poor means lacking sufficient money to live at a standard considered comfortable or normal in society.

Being poor is a state of being, not a mindset. Being poor causes one to be humble. And of course being poor is only one aspect of this scripture because being honest is necessary to keep yourself from experiencing the worst the world has to offer. It would be bad to be poor and dishonest, God wouldn't be pleased.

To be rich is not always a blessing especially depending on how one became rich. To be rich and dishonest would definitely make you a fool and would appear to God as being ungrateful and the path you travel would not be blessed, you may still receive grace and mercy.

24:28 "Don't testify against your neighbors without cause, don't lie about them.

This scripture is clear and plain, and not much room for misinterpretation. Speak truthfully regarding others, so that bad seed is not sown on your behalf. If the truth is not known then say nothing or at the least admit to not knowing the truth.

26:12 "Do you see a man(who is unteachable) wise in his own eyes and full of self-conceit? These is more hope for a food than for him."

This scripture speaks to how one views themselves and why. To be unteachable in itself means you are unwise. To think too highly of oneself isn't wise and shows you are full of conceit. A fool is someone who acts unwisely and silly according to this scripture for this individual there is hope. A fool can be taught or shown differently and change allowing God to have his way with that person and their life. Having hope is necessary. Hope is defined as a feeling of expectation and desire for a certain thing to happen. Why would anyone want to live without hope?

Isaiah

29:13-15 "And so the Lord says, "These people say they are mine. They honor me with their lips, but their hearts are far from me. And their worship of me is nothing but man-made rules learned by mechanical or habitual repetition. Because of this, I will once again astound these hypocrites with amazing wonders. The wisdom of the wise will pass away, and the intelligence of the intelligent will disappear." What sorrow awaits those who try to hide their plans from the LORD, who do their evil deeds in the dark! "The LORD can't see us," they say. "He doesn't know what's going on!"

Now this is some good Word, I love the book of Isaiah. In this scripture the Lord is not fooled by people who claim they are his and believe, but only shows it through what they say or claim with no actions or behaviors to support what they say to be true. There is no honor to God if it's not flowing from your heart. The worship of these individuals is nothing but religion, which is the act of being spiritual. Going through the motions of worship because someone taught you isn't the same as worshipping God with YOUR WHOLE HEART, mind, body, spirit, and soul. Despite all this God continues to surprise us with amazing wonders often playing out as grace and mercy given.

But even so there are still consequences the wise will no longer be wise, the intelligent will no longer be intelligent.

Sadness and unexpected ends await those who attempt to hide or deceive God about the plans and the intent behind their evil deeds done in the dark.

God knows and sees all despite their unbelief that God could see them and doesn't quite know what's going on. God is El Roi (The God who sees). God is omnipotent and omniscience (all knowing meaning God knows everything, including the past, present, and the future. God is omnipresent (all present).

Do not be deceive by what is assumed due to lack of sight or disbelief in who God is and all he can do. He is all-powerful, all knowing, and all present.

<u>Jeremiah</u>

7:1-11 "The LORD gave another message to Jeremiah. He said, "Go to the entrance of the LORD's Temple, and give this message to the people: 'O Judah, listen to this message from the LORD! Listen to it, all of you who worship here! This is what the LORD of Heaven's Armies, the God of Israel, says: "'Even now, if you quit your evil ways, I will let you stay in your own land. But don't be fooled by those who promise you safety simply because the LORD's Temple is here. They chant, "The LORD's Temple is here! The LORD's Temple is here!" But I will be merciful only if you stop your evil thoughts and deeds and start treating each other with justice; only if you stop exploiting foreigners, orphans, and widows; only if you stop your murdering; and only if you stop harming yourselves by worshiping idols. Then I will let you stay in this land that I gave to your ancestors to keep forever.

"'Don't be fooled into thinking that you will never suffer because the Temple is here. It is a lie! Do you really think you can steal; murder, commit adultery, lie, and burn incense to Baal and all those other new gods of yours, and then come here and stand before me in my Temple and chant, "We are safe!"—only to go right back to all those evils again? Don't you yourselves admit that this Temple, which bears my name, has become a den of thieves? Surely, I see all the evil going on there. I, the LORD, have spoken!

Praise God for this scripture, he can't be fooled or deceived. God sent one of the major Prophets to relay his important message to his people of Judah.

Jeremiah accepted the assignment (obedience) and went before the people as a willing vessel.

God is awesome with instructing us, guiding us, correcting us, and warning us. More often than not, we ignore all of the above then blame God because things did not turn out as we like or hope. Word and instruction is given, our job is to choose to obey and trust the outcome sometime not knowing what the outcome is.

In these instructions God was plain, clear, firm and direct. God saw the evil, and inappropriate behavior, but also knew their desires for safety would be rewarded by God only if they took heed to his instructions, guidance, warning, and corrections.

God told the people to quit being evil and doing evil deeds and if they obey, God would allow them to stay in their own land. He warns them to not be fooled by the presence of the Lord's Temple. God was letting them know their presence and entry in temple will not protect or keep them safe, they must change their behavior and act accordingly, to receive and be under God mighty arm of protection. He warns of not being fooled that the Lord's Temple is Holy and Blessed but wrong and evil doings voids God's protection, disobedience and deception lead to their own destruction and downfall.

God lets them know that if they turn from their evil thoughts and deed AND:

- Start treating each other with justice
- Only if you stop exploiting foreigners, orphans, widows
- Only if you stop your murdering
- Only if you stop harming yourselves by worshipping idols.

God uses the verbiage "Only if" to show that these directives are a must and non-negotiable

If all these things are obeyed then and only then will God allow them to stay in the land that their ancestors were given by God to keep forever.

God was specific and warned the people that suffering is still a possibility if their behavior is not corrected. The presence of the temple isn't enough.

He questions their intent as they enter the temple, considering the stealing, murdering, adultery, lying, and worshipping of other God's was the behavior they displayed, only to claim safety as they stand before God knowing the wrongs committed outside the walls of the temple. Your intent behind your actions make your presence in the temple rewarding.

God boldly lets them know he see them and can't be fooled. He sent Jeremiah in hopes that the people will take heed.

We must learn to take God at his Word. Trust his instructions as they are for our good and the benefit of the kingdom of God.

17:9 "The heart is deceitful above all things and it is extremely sick; who can understand it fully and know its secret motives."

This scripture speaks of the heart which can be easily misled by emotions and the rising of our flesh. Our heart and the feeling and desires that flow from it depending on what in our heart and it can be deceitful and a vehicle for sowing bad seed. The scripture has determined for us that no one can understand the heart fully and know its secret motives.

The Truth based on Scripture from the New Testament

Matthew

6:24 "No one can serve two masters. For you will hate one and love the other; you will be devoted to one and despise the other. You cannot serve God and be enslaved to money.

This scripture is often misstated, misunderstood, and misinterpreted. Master is defined as a man who has people working for him, especially servants or slaves.

As a servant of God who is my Master, I understand that to worship God wholeheartedly is the only way to please God. There are truly only two masters to consider God or Satan. Yes, I love God and I absolutely hate the devil. I do not entertain the devil or his attempts to steal, kill, or destroy my life, future, and that of my family.

If you truly love God, and believe in his Word, the devil and his ways will have and should have no bearing on your life.

To be devoted to God speaks to having a heart for God, who he is and his impact on your life. When one is devoted, they are loving, loyal, steadfast, and unmovable and cannot be deterred. This devotion to God makes it easy to despise the devil and all he brings. One is good and one is evil. One has our best interest at heart and the other wants nothing more than to destroy and cancel the assignment on our life, given by God.

The last sentence of this scripture is plain, and it cant be misinterpreted. You cant serve God and be money drive or motivated. Money or the chase of money will mislead you and cause you to go off course. God's plan for us does not include chasing money, but he blesses us with opportunities of great provision when you trust him to be your source and seek him 1st in all things.

If you choose to accept the position God designed for you, the provision will come.

6:33 "Seek the kingdom of God above all else and live righteously and he will give you everything you need."

To remain on track and in the Will of God, requires you seek God and his kingdom above all else. Your greatest desire should be to see God in all things, to experience him, and to seek and reside in his kingdom, where he has purposed you.

God wants us to live righteously and in return he will give us everything we need.

Everything we need is given, just for doing the right thing at all times were be provided by God. He is just that Good to us.

Do right and he will take care of you.

It is our choice to choose to do the right thing.

You always have a choice. Seek God and you won't be misled.

7:1-5 "Do not judge others, and you will not be judged. For you will be treated as you treat others. The standard you use in judging is the standard by which you will be judged. "And why worry about a speck in your friend's eye when you have a log in your own? How can you think of saying to your friend, 'Let me help you get rid of that speck in your eye,' when you can't see past the log in your own eye? Hypocrite! First get rid of the log in your own eye; then you will see well enough to deal with the speck in your friend's eye.

We have all been guilty of this at some point in our Christian walk and spiritual journey. Once you understand this scripture, you see yourself, others, and their view of you differently. We often look at others wondering why they do what they do or why they are doing things differently or better.

This scripture tell us to not look at what others are doing and decide if they are right or wrong based on our view. Our view is always distorted if we are not seeing through God's eyes.

We can't look at what others do without considering every aspect of their lives such as :

- How they were born
- How the pregnancy went
- Parents upbringing
- Home environment
- Traumatic events
- Peer circle

So much determines who we are, why we do what we do, how we go about doing thing, etc. The things listed are the things that help shape who we are and our character, morals, values, standards, and boundaries.

God specifies in the Bible in a number of different ways to do unto others, as you would have them do unto you. God advises us that how we treat others is how we will be treated in return. Same as reaping what you sow.

The common mistake that most people make is that they tend to judge people unfairly or on a tilted scale. Most of the time they are judged in a way that you don't even judge yourself. If everyone judged themselves the way they judge others, no one would bother with the latter.

When you judge your own actions and behaviors according to God, God's will, and His Word you tend to have compassion for those whom others may judge.

Most miss the mark because they judge others based on the world's standard, which unfortunately is not based on God or His Word and will cause one to do more harm than good.

In this scripture, God actually questions why one would look at another's shortcomings, flaws, and imperfections when everyone has shortcomings, flaws, and all were created imperfect.

The bonus is God has never required perfection from us, so we should not expect or look for it in others. You can't help others if you can't see thing as God does. Your attempt to judge, correct, or help someone based on you, your view, and your knowledge is a set up and will definitely be bad seed sown for both parties to reap.

Our goal should be to see others as God does, having the mind of Christ.

To judge or look at the wrongs of others when you were created imperfect, you too will do wrong or sin. How can you see the wrongs of others while you have done your own wrongs?

Most feel if they did not do the wrong they are judging someone else for doing, they are somehow better or above the other.

God sees all wrongs as being wrong; no sin is greater. Sin is sin. Wrong is wrong.

Some even split hairs by determining if the wrong has a victim.

But even with that thought you must consider that all sin and wrong doing have victims whether it's the person committing the sin or wrong doing or the person it was committed against.

Once you experience this reality check; you become mindful of you, your mind, and you own behavior and actions making sure that that are aligned with God's Word and his Will for your life, then and only then will you be of any help.

7:15-20(The Tree and its Fruit) "Beware of false prophets who come disguised as harmless sheep but are really vicious wolves. You can identify them by their fruit, that is, by the way they act. Can you pick grapes from thorn bushes, or figs from thistles? A good tree produces good fruit, and a bad tree produces bad fruit. A good tree cannot produce bad fruit, and a bad tree cannot produce good fruit. So, every tree that does not produce good fruit is chopped down and thrown into the fire. Yes, just as you can identify a tree by its fruit, so you can identify people by their actions.

This scripture serves as a visual of how God sees us. We were born to be good trees producing good fruit. Its takes life choices and different experiences to change a good tree to a bad tree producing bad fruit, while sowing bad seed.

Initially this scripture starts with a warning, to beware of false prophets. A prophet is a person regarded as an inspired teacher or proclaimer of the Will of God. We should definitely be aware of anyone acting falsely in this capacity. False Prophets appear to be harmless; but do not be deceived. To act in this manner is actually considered vicious. Vicious can be defined as being deliberately cruel or violent, which signifies the extent of the possible damage a False Prophet can do.

Believe it or not a False Prophet can be identified by the fruit they produce or by the way they act.

A good tree will always produce good fruit.

A bad tree will always produce bad fruit.

It is impossible for a bad tree to produce good fruit from bad seed.

This scripture also advises that every tree that does not produce good fruit is chopped down and thrown into the fire. Praise God!!!!!

Reminder: You can identify a tree by its fruit, and the same goes for people. You can also identify people by their actions, behaviors, words, and works.

Stay Woke!

Pay Attention!!

Avoid Distractions!!!

7:21-23 (true disciples) "Not everyone who calls out to me, 'Lord! Lord!' will enter the Kingdom of Heaven. Only those who actually do the will of my Father in heaven will enter. On judgment day, many will say to me, 'Lord! Lord! We prophesied in your name and cast out demons in your name and performed many miracles in your name.' But I will reply, 'I never knew you. Get away from me, you who break God's laws.'

God gives us so much in his Word to instruct and protect is, only if we would take heed. He tells us that just because we call on his name doesn't mean we will enter the Kingdom of Heaven. The way to enter heaven is to actually do the Will of God..... PERIOD. These is no gray area.

Live a life pleasing to God, Be a willing vessel!!!!

Rule breakers will not be happy on judgment day, despite their claims of right doing.

God know all, sees all, and will not be deceived by lying lips.

He will demand that they remove themselves from his presence.

15:18-19"But the words you speak come from the heart-that is what defines you. For from the heart comes evil thoughts, murder, adultery, all sexual immorality, theft, lying, and slander."

God assures us all through the bible about our tongue, the words we speak, our heart behind the actions and words, OUR Intent.....What you speak flows from you heart. What comes from your mouth proceeds the heart; and this action causes a person to be defiled.

Based on the conditions of your heart, it can lead one to evil thoughts, murder, adultery, sexual immorality, theft, false witness, and slander.

Guard your heart!!!

Mark

7:20-23 "And then he added, "It is what comes from inside that defiles you. For from within, out of a person's heart, come evil thoughts, sexual immorality, theft, murder, adultery, greed, wickedness, deceit, lustful desires, envy, slander, pride, and foolishness. All these vile things come from within; they are what defile you."

God is letting us know that what flows from within causes us to be defiled. I know you are thinking....Inside. In your heart, not your mind or body. The things listed in the scripture of what comes from within ones heart are the very things that will defile you

10:19 "But to answer your question, you know the commandments: 'You must not murder. You must not commit adultery. You must not steal. You must not testify falsely. You must not cheat anyone. Honor your father and mother.'"

This is God giving us the basic instruction to stay out of trouble and breaking laws that will cause us to experience things God never intended, or the consequences of all the wrongs mentioned. Follow this scripture and you will avoid a lot of the devils pitfalls while remaining in good standing with God.

12:31 "The 2nd commandment is equally important: Love your neighbor as yourself. No other commandment is greater than these."

Love is one of the most important things God instructs us to do, it is vital to our walk and how we impact those whose paths we cross.

Love conquers all

Love never FAILS.......

Luke

6:31 "Treat others the same way you want them to treat you."

This is a simple command people often times struggle with because they treat people the way people treat them which normally is referred to as bad or at least not the way one wants to be treated. Manifesting as "get back or revenge, which in itself is wrong because God says in Romans 12:17-18 "Never repay anyone evil for evil. Take thought for what is right, gracious, and proper in the sight of everyone. If possible, as far as, it depends on you live at peace with everyone.

The initial scriptures wants us to treat others the way God says no matter what they do. Expect people to treat you the way God planned and if they do not, you pray for them.

Do not allow others to have more control of your actions and behavior than God. Please God in all that you do and trust God to protect you from evil known and unknown.

6:38 "Give and you will receive. Your gift will return to you in full—pressed down, shaken together to make room for more, running over, and poured into your lap. The amount you give will determine the amount you get back."

This is a scripture that often makes me shout, but it's also the one my spirit man refers to when giving or doing for others is on my heart. A lot of church's reference this scripture when its time for tithes and offering. This scripture speaks to the giver, to those with a giving heart not for credit or accolades.

When you have a heart for Christ, a heart of giving will manifest within you and great and plentiful is your reward.

16:1-2 "Jesus told this story to his disciples: "There was a certain rich man who had a manager handling his affairs. One day a report came that the manager was wasting his employer's money. So the employer called him in and said, 'What's this I hear about you? Get your report in order, because you are going to be fired.'"

This scripture is a bold view of wrong doers being punished for abusing their power and position and being wasteful of all the things God has approved. Basically, if you are hired or chose for a job or position do right by those that believe in you enough to bless you with an opportunity.

If you not, you can lose the position or be fired but will be known as wasteful and cannot be trusted to do right with what God saw fit to give.

16:10-12 "If you are faithful in little things, you will be faithful in large ones. But if you are dishonest in little things, you won't be honest with greater responsibilities. And if you are untrustworthy about worldly wealth, who will trust you with the true riches of heaven? And if you are not faithful with other people's things, why should you be trusted with things of your own?"

I love how the bible will use different examples to ensure the point being made is clear. This scripture always keep me grounded and humble. It explains how God's mind works. We must prove ourselves good in all ways, circumstances, and situations. Key is doing good or right no matter what because God is always watching he cant be deceived.

Operate in life and in this world, as if God is always watching us to see if we are acting and behaving accordingly and doing what is pleasing in his sight.

At all times – It is never ok to something bad or against the Word of God.

God sees all!

God knows all!

19:9-14 "Then Jesus told this story to some who had great confidence in their own righteousness and scorned everyone else: "Two men went to the Temple to pray. One was a Pharisee, and the other was a despised tax collector. The Pharisee stood by himself and prayed this prayer: 'I thank you, God, that I am not like other people—cheaters, sinners, adulterers. I am certainly not like that tax collector! I fast twice a week, and I give you a tenth of my income.' "But the tax collector stood at a distance and dared not even lift his eyes to heaven as he prayed. Instead, he beat his chest in sorrow, saying, 'O God, be merciful to me, for I am a sinner.' 14 I tell you, this sinner, not the Pharisee, returned home justified before God. For those who exalt themselves will be humbled, and those who humble themselves will be exalted."

Jesus had a way of telling stories to warn or advise us through situations and circumstances we can relate too.

This story speaks about 2 different men based on who they were called or labeled as. Pharisee was characterized as a self righteous person or hypocrite. The character of a Pharisee is opposite of that of a collector. In this scripture God points out how the character of one person is considered to be above or better than another because of occupation or status.

The Pharisee believes they always operate in right standing but because the do the things that those who are thought to be less than do they are better.

That thought in itself displeases God. God knows no one is perfect and to believe one is perfect while pointing out the imperfections of another.

God would prefer be in the presence of someone who knows who they are and able to admit they are a sinner and repent asking him for mercy. Because of the heart of the tax collector, he is justified before God.

For individuals who are held in high regard will be humbled, and those who humble themselves will be held in a high regard.

John

8:32 "And you will know the Truth, and the truth will set you free."

This scripture is often misinterpreted, most say the truth will set you, but knowing the truth is what sets us free.

Operating in God's truth which is the Word of God will allow you to be free.

True freedom is being who God created you to be according to the Word, God's plan and purpose for your life unhindered by this world, their standards and ideals that often keep up bound and unable to be free and act as God intended.

God's Word is truth and to know it and operate from it as truth, guidance, and instructions will free us and allow us to experience life on God's terms.

8:44 "For you are the children of your father the devil, and you love to do the evil things he does. He was a murderer from the beginning. He has always hated the truth, because there is no truth in him. When he lies, it is consistent with his character; for he is a liar and the father of lies.

In this scripture, Jesus is educating a group of people who are not who they say they are and believe otherwise. He lets them know that because they have not followed his example and instead tried to kill him because he told them the truth, which came from God the Father. Jesus tell them that because of their behavior, their father is Satan and they love to do as he does. He warns that the devil was always a murderer, and always hated the truth because he knows no truth and there is none in him. When Satan opens his mouth and act according to his will it is always consistent with who he really is.

Lying is a characteristic of the devil. Satan is the Father of lies.

14:6 "Jesus told him, "I am the way, the truth, and the life. No one can come to the Father except through me."

This scripture has carried a variety of meaning for me over the years as I have progressed through my spiritual walk and journey.

When Jesus says he is the way, he simply means if you do as I have done and follow his example you will live a life of truth and be led by the truth in all that, you do which leads to us living a life God intended for us to have and experience.

He solidified this message by letting us know this is the only way and no exceptions for anyone.

In Romans 2:11 "For there is no respect of persons"

God is no respecter of persons, he treats everyone the same and expected to live by the same standard as Jesus. No one is exempt.

16:13 "When the spirit of truth comes, he will guide you into all truth. He will not speak on his own but will tell you what he has heard. He will tell you about the future."

This scripture talks about the Holy Spirit. The most awesome gift from God to help lead and guide us in a life of truth, and that is truth in **all things**.

So we seek God 1st in all things and the Holy Spirit will lead us in truth in all things.

Key things to carry with you no matter what it can help put and keep things in perspective.

Acts

3:19-21 "Now repent of your sins and turn to God, so that your sins may be wiped away. Then times of refreshment will come from the presence of the Lord, and he will again send you Jesus, your appointed Messiah. For he must remain in heaven until the time for the final restoration of all things, as God promised long ago through his holy prophets."

Praise God for this scripture, I love the scriptures that make it plain and gives clear instructions and the reward for adhering.

God tells us he knows we are sinners but sin can be wiped away by confessing or repenting of the sins and turning to God. These actions lead to the wiping away of sins.

Praise God Hallelujah!!!!

The presence of God!!!! To be in his presence is like nothing else that you could ever feel. As we turn away from our repented sins and turn toward God and act and do according to his Will we will find ourselves in his presence experiencing times if refreshment and he will send his son again.

God will send his son back at the appointed time; until the time of final restoration of all things.

5:1-11 "But there was a certain man named Ananias who, with his wife, Sapphira, sold some property. He brought part of the money to the apostles, claiming it was the full amount. With his wife's consent, he kept the rest. Then Peter said, "Ananias, why have you let Satan fill your heart? You lied to the Holy Spirit, and you kept some of the money for yourself. The property was yours to sell or not sell, as you wished. And after selling it, the money was also yours to give away. How could you do a thing like this? You weren't lying to us but to God!" As soon as Ananias heard these words, he fell to the floor and died. Everyone who heard about it was terrified. Then some young men got up, wrapped him in a sheet, and took him out and buried him. About three hours later his wife came in, not knowing what had happened. Peter asked her, "Was this the price you and your husband received for your land?" "Yes," she replied, "that was the price." And Peter said, "How could the two of you even think of conspiring to test the Spirit of the Lord like this? The young men who buried your husband are just outside the door, and they will carry you out, too." Instantly, she fell to the floor and died. When the young men came in and saw that she was dead, they carried her out and buried her beside her husband. Great fear gripped the entire church and everyone else who heard what had happened."

This is a story of deception and truth and someone standing in deception when the truth is known. This is something we have all encountered in some capacity.

This story starts with a sell of property and the owner received the full amount, but got his wife to agree to lie and say they did not get the full amount.

His wife consented to him keeping the rest and they only took part of the money to the apostles.

The apostles knew that he was not being truthful. Peter asked bluntly "why have you let satan fill your heart?

As I stated in prior pages our wrongs and sins flow from the heart and defiles us. Therefore, when we do wrong or not do as God says it is because the devil has somehow talked us or charmed us away from the truth.

He lied about his blessings, which in this scripture was equivalent to lying to the Holy Spirit and kept what God said to give.

Have you ever been guilty of that?

There was no reason to lie. The property was his to sell and the money was his to give or keep. The issue here is the unnecessary lie and joint deception. They had deceit in their heart, and the devil was behind their actions.

This kind of lie is really more to God.

The intent to give all was not heart felt or his true desire. He wanted God to believe he was giving all he received.

The lied (unnecessarily), it was unwarranted.

Because of the actions and intent Ananias died immediately after he was told he lied to God. The fact that he died for something so avoidable instead of speaking the truth and having honest intentions, the people became terrified at what occurred.

Peter even gave the wife another chance to be honest and still chose deception.

This lie tested the spirit of the Lord!!

Because she still chose to lie, her death followed and she was buried with her husband.

In our own personal walk no matter the connection, we all have the chance and choice to do the right thing and tell the truth.

Romans

3:23 "For everyone has sinned; we all fall short of God's glory."

This scripture reminds us that no one is perfect, and it is not required.

God knows ALL.......

He's never surprised by the choices we make.

12:2 "And do not be conformed to this world but be transformed *and* progressively changed by the renewing of your mind, so that you may prove [for yourselves] what the will of God is, that which is good and acceptable and perfect."

This is one of my guiding scriptures; it helps me determine what to do in a number of situations. This means do not let this world be the deciding factor. Allow the Word of God to lead you in your life choices. This world is corrupt and if you are led by corruption, you too are corrupt.

Living according to the Word leads to a life of righteousness.

The Word of God is our life instruction guide. Knowing and living according to it, and believing it as truth will transform you and progressively change you by constantly renewing your mind with God's Words. God is your creator and the creator of all things. God created you for a purpose and a plan.

Our lives and the results there of is visual proof or is suppose to be visible proof of who God is, his existence, and his Will for each of us, this world, and the kingdom of God's.

The Word of God leads us in all things that are good, what is acceptable, and perfect according to God.

13:11-14 "This is all the more urgent, for you know how late it is; time is running out. Wake up, for our salvation is nearer now than when we first believed. The night is almost gone; the day of salvation will soon be here. So remove your dark deeds like dirty clothes, and put on the shining armor of right living. Because we belong to the day, we must live decent lives for all to see. Don't participate in the darkness of wild parties and drunkenness, or in sexual promiscuity and immoral living, or in quarreling and jealousy. Instead, clothe yourself with the presence of the Lord Jesus Christ. And don't let yourself think about ways to indulge your evil desires."

There are several scriptures that serve as wake up calls; packed with truths, directives, and guidance, and this is one of them.

This is about the urgency of getting our life and behavior in order and in line with God, His Word, and His Will.

We have all heard that salvation is closer than we may think.

But we all know that only God knows the appointed time of all things.

As mentioned in Matthew 24:36 "However no one knows the day or hour when these things will happen, not even the angels in heaven or the Son himself. Only the Father knows!"

We are instructed or guided in this scripture to turn from our dark deeds, and turn to the light.

Because we are seen in the light it is there where we must be seen living honestly, properly, and honorably. We must avoid behaviors done in the dark with the intent to be hidden, to be a deceiver of truth or righteousness.

Avoid darkness and the things done and accepted in the darkness including drunkenness, improper sexual behaviors, living outside of the rules of the Word of God, which is equivalent to immoral living and fighting which is never condoned, and jealousy, which shows you're unsatisfied, and refusal to accept who you are and who God created you to be.

God would prefer us engulf ourselves in who Jesus Christ was and is and follow his examples, and refuse to allow your mind to think or concede, indulge in any evil thing ir respond or cater to any evil desire.

Be mindful of what is leading and guiding you.

14:1 "Accept other believers who are weak in faith, and don't argue with them about what they think is right or wrong."

As children of God, we are to accept all believer no matter the strength of their faith. There are levels to the spiritual walk and no two spiritual walks or journeys are the same.

God intentionally made them all different expecting our coming together to be an iron sharpens iron type of relationship.

And there is never a reason to argue about right and wrong because right and truth stands alone and need no help it is lies, wrong that require explanation and justification.

There is no gray area. That is where people reside when they find it difficult to do what is right in heart and according to God and His Word, and reference misinformation, unhealed situations, and operating from a broken place somehow within them to justify them not choosing to do and be as the Word of God and the Holy Spirit leads us to.

16:17-18 "And now I make one more appeal, my dear brothers and sisters. Watch out for people who cause divisions and upset people's faith by teaching things contrary to what you have been taught. Stay away from them. Such people are not serving Christ our Lord; they are serving their own personal interests. By smooth talk and glowing words, they deceive innocent people.

Some writers of the bible had the job of addressing the people with passion, plead, and appeals to get them to do what God's Word instructs.

Paul in this scripture warns us of who to look out for as well as their motivation and intentions.

Beware of naysayers, hell raisers, devil's advocates, and people who don't believe in God, His Word, and His Will.

They intentionally us contrary beliefs to divide and disprove what God has taught us.

Do not be deceived these are not servants of Christ our Lord, they serve their own personal interest and that of the Devil.

There is no splitting hairs, you are a believer and with God or you are not. This is not in reference to a backslider or someone who is walking their spiritual walk. But still have difficulties.

This refers to people who have chosen not to believe and their thoughts, actions, and behaviors support that sentiment.

This is why we must know the Word of God for ourselves, so we will be armed with one of the most mightiest weapons! The Word of God.......

1 Corinthians

6:9-11 "Don't you realize that those who do wrong will not inherit the Kingdom of God? Don't fool yourselves. Those who indulge in sexual sin, or who worship idols, or commit adultery, or are male prostitutes, or practice homosexuality, or are thieves, or greedy people, or drunkards, or are abusive, or cheat people—none of these will inherit the Kingdom of God. Some of you were once like that. But you were cleansed; you were made holy; you were made right with God by calling on the name of the Lord Jesus Christ and by the Spirit of our God."

Some of you were once like that, but you were cleansed; you were made holy, you were made right with God by calling on the name of the Lord Jesus Christ and by the Spirit of our God.

This scripture is one that initially scared me because of the list of things that would have or could keep me and those I know from inheriting the kingdom of God.

Praise God for his grace and mercy and our ability to repent, confess, and turn away from things we once did or believed was against God.

Hallelujah we are made clean!!!

Clean, Holy, made right with God all by "CALLING on the name of the Lord Jesus Christ and by the Spirit of our God."

Take heed to the Word of God, accept it as truth and instruction and what his Word manifest in your life and the lives of others whom you impact.

2 Corinthians

4:4 "Satan, who is the god of this world, has blinded he minds of those who don't believe. They are unable to see the glorious light of the Good news. They do not understand this message about the glory of Christ who is the exact likeness of God."

This was an informative scripture that brings "This world into perspective for those who understand the supernatural realm and the difference of living and residing and being of this world versus living in this world but reside and operate from the supernatural realm.

Do not conform to the world it will always lead you away from God, His Word and His Will for your life, your fture, and your family.

This world means you no good and its primary goal is to lable, confine, control, and use for a greater purpose that will only serve satan and his agenda to kill, steal, and destroy God's plan.

Any non-believer makes themselves vulnerable to the devil, his tricks, charm and evil ways. Non-believers can be deceived and blended. He has many ways to continue to case one not to believe. He prevents them from being able to see God or his light, and hear his Word let alone be affected by these things. They

do not understand the Glory of Christ who is the exact likeness of God.

11:3 "But I fear that somehow your pure and undivided devotion to Christ will be corrupted, just as Eve was deceived by the cunning ways of the serpent."

The fear in this scripture I feel is coming to those who accept that calling and decide to begin their spiritual walk and journey.

God gives us all the Word to protect and guide us so we can fulfill our role in the kingdom of God. But this scripture reminds us that the devil has been corrupting God's creation since the beginning of time despite the creators efforts to create pure and undivided followers. The devil is still at work and as believers we must remember that the victory is already ours, and we must learn and began to walk and operate from a place of victory.

11:13-15 "These people are false apostles. They are deceitful workers who disguise themselves as apostles of Christ. But I am not surprised! Even Satan disguises himself as an angel of light. So it is no wonder that his servants also disguise themselves as servants of righteousness. In the end, they will get the punishment their wicked deeds deserve."

There is no coincidence that as we cover deception the false apostle or people pretending to be someone they are not with the intent to mislead or throw another person of course affect any life committed.

This is the cleverness of the devil.

One of the devils tricks is to use people whether willing or not to negatively affect other who have willingly chosen God but struggles as we all do.

People who falsely pretend to be someone who is fulfilling the calling from God set out to defraud many people on behalf of Satan.

I can't stand the devil!!!!

His soldiers do as he does and praise God that they too shall be punished for their evil and wicked deeds and ways.

Galatians

5:16-26(Living by the Spirit's Power) "So I say, let the Holy Spirit guide your lives. Then you won't be doing what your sinful nature craves. The sinful nature wants to do evil, which is just the opposite of what the Spirit wants. And the Spirit gives us desires that are the opposite of what the sinful nature desires. These two forces are constantly fighting each other, so you are not free to carry out your good intentions. But when you are directed by the Spirit, you are not under obligation to the law of Moses. When you follow the desires of your sinful nature, the results are very clear: sexual immorality, impurity, lustful pleasures, idolatry, sorcery, hostility, quarreling, jealousy, outbursts of anger, selfish ambition, dissension, division, envy, drunkenness, wild parties, and other sins like these. Let me tell you again, as I have before, that anyone living that sort of life will not inherit the Kingdom of God. But the Holy Spirit produces this kind of fruit in our lives: love, joy, peace, patience, kindness, goodness, faithfulness, gentleness, and self-control. There is no law against these things! Those who belong to Christ Jesus have nailed the passions and desires of their sinful nature to his cross and crucified them there. Since we are living by the Spirit, let us follow the Spirit's leading in every part of our lives. Let us not become conceited, provoke one another, or be jealous of one another."

When you are directed by the Spirit, you are not under obligation to the law of Moses. When you follow the desires of your sinful nature, the results are very clear:

- sexual immorality
- impurity
- lustful pleasures
- idolatry
- sorcery
- hostility
- quarreling
- jealousy
- outbursts of anger
- selfish ambition
- dissension
- division
- envy
- drunkenness
- wild parties
- and other sins like these

Let me tell you again, as I have before, that anyone living that sort of life will not inherit the Kingdom of God.

But the Holy Spirit produces this kind of fruit in our lives:

- Love
- Joy
- Peace
- Patience
- Kindness
- Goodness

- Faithfulness
- Gentleness
- self-control

There are no laws against these things.

Those who belong to Christ Jesus have nailed the passions and desires of their sinful nature to his cross and crucified them there. Since we are living by the spirit, let us follow the spirits leading in every part if our lives. Let us not become conceited or provoke one another, or be jealous of one another.

The Holy Spirit is very important to every child of God whether they know it or believe it or not. One of God's greatest gifts that defies all logic but both required and necessary.

The greatest thing about the Holy Spirit and its leading is it guides our lives, and directs us away from the devil. Our sinful natures which serves our flesh, and emotions both of which must come to a point where they are submitted to your spirit man to ensure you are living according to the Word and your life is aligned with God's Will for you.

Our sinful nature serves the sinner within us that prompts is to act against God committing evil deeds, and willing doing wrong. This is opposite of what the spirit will lead you to and away from.

The Holy Spirit can even lead us by giving us desires that are opposite from the sinful natures desires.

These two things are used by their creator as a part of the God vs Satan war.

God sent and uses the Holy Spirit to guide us and lead us according to the Word of God, God's Will, and plan for the kingdom of God, and his people.

Satan sends and uses our sinful nature, which feeds off the sinner's minds within you. The sinner within us is motivated by our flesh and emotions often times being controlled by the devil and the spirit man is often bound and gagged when we allow the sinner within us and flesh to be our guide.

Living a life with the Holy Spirit being our guide leading us accordingly, is the most freeing thing you can experience.

True freedom is living according to the Word, and it can be obtained and maintained.

There is no freedom when our flesh is in charge

There is no freedom if our sinful nature is leading our charge. This will make you a slave to sin.

The Holy Spirit is all about good intentions and the intent behind the actions is always important.

The power that flows from the Holy Spirit is great and mighty and when we are being guided by the Holy Spirit we are not under obligation to the law of Moses(1st 5 books of the bible).

The sinful nature undoubtedly will result in the things listed in the scripture(19-21), but it also means they will not inherit the kingdom of God.

The Holy Spirit and the presence of this being brings so much more when added to a person, situation, circumstances, or lives.

The kind of fruit produced by the Holy Spirit's presence is part of what makes it such a great gift.

These are the things people go to extraordinary lengths to obtain not realizing the Holy Spirit is key.

Key to receiving and experiencing love, joy, peace, patience, kindness, goodness, faithfulness, gentleness, and self-control. THERE IS NO LAW AGAINST THESE THINGS................!

Another great thing is that once we choose God and we then belong to Christ. At that point, our passions and desires will be nailed to the cross with Jesus. From henceforward we will be living according to the Spirit, choosing to follow the Holy Spirit in every part of our lives.

We must be careful to not get puffed up, proud or conceited, and don't go against your sisters and brothers who walk this walk and beware of jealousy that can be perceived by God as ungratefulness and you not trust who God created you to be.

6:1-3(We harvest what we plant) "Dear brothers and sisters, if another believer is overcome by some sin, you who are godly should gently and humbly help that person back onto the right path. And be careful not to fall into the same temptation yourself. Share each other's burdens, and in this way obey the law of Christ. If you think you are too important to help someone, you are only fooling yourself. You are not that important."

This is what sadly isn't done, but needs to be something we all do. When we see someone struggling in a manner in which we have already overcome, we meet them with compassion because you have an understanding because you were once where they are.

The things we go through and overcome are not just for us, but it's for those who will go through similar or familiar situations.

We can and should help them find their way and get back on track.

Make sure your spiritual strength is intact and weapons on deck to ensure you don't fall prey to temptations or any vices.

Share your stories! The how, why, what, and when..... Sharing helps others know that overcoming is possible. Just knowing a person can overcome without knowing what they had to do to overcome takes away from the purpose and meaning of it all.

 Never be above reproach. We should always be willing to help others who are walking their walk despite it not looking like they think it should. We are to be who God called us to be to others.

6:7-8 "Don't be misled—you cannot mock the justice of God. You will always harvest what you plant. Those who live only to satisfy their own sinful nature will harvest decay and death from that sinful nature. But those who live to please the Spirit will harvest everlasting life from the Spirit."

Covering the topic of deception has been so eye opening. Once again we look at a scripture that warns us not to be misled. This scripture reiterates that God is a God of justice and can't be mocked nor fooled.

God tells us that what we plant we will harvest. This has also been stated differently as "you reap what you sow".

Those who operate from their sinful nature they will harvest, according to that same nature.

Those who operate from the leading of the Holy Spirit live to please God, reaping the harvest of ever-lasting life.

Ephesians

2:1-3 "Once you were dead because of your disobedience and your many sins. You used to live in sin, just like the rest of the world, obeying the devil—the commander of the powers in the unseen world. He is the spirit at work in the hearts of those who refuse to obey God. All of us used to live that way, following the passionate desires and inclinations of our sinful nature. By our very nature, we were subject to God's anger, just like everyone else."

This scripture is one reason why we cant judge anyone else's walk or the timing in which one decides to choose God and change.

Before we chose God and chose to believe that Jesus Christ died on the cross for our sins, we chose to live according to our flesh, our emotions, and our sinful nature which are controlled by the devil when they aren't fully submitted to your Spirit.

Living in sin is the equivalent of living in death. Living in sin means we are living disobedient to God and his Word and not help the kingdom of God as God intended for all his children.

Whenever we refuse to obey God have no doubt that the devil is behind that decision, and the devils spirit is at work in your heart.

We have all done this at some point in our own walk but this isn't the end and things will turn as you turn away from the sin, and help your flesh and emotions to submit to your spirit man. Refuse to be led by sinful nature but live a life that is led by the Holy Spirit, which has some assurances for you as you embrace your process of becoming who God created you to be.

Refuse to live a life apart from God where you are led by the Holy Spirit and freely doing everything God created you to do, becoming everything God created you to become, experiencing everything God planned, and receiving everything God promise you would receive.

Life begins when you choose God and choose life according to his word fulfilling your purpose within his plan for the Kingdom of God.

4:1-6(Unity in the Body) (Unity of the Spirit) "Therefore I, a prisoner for serving the Lord, beg you to lead a life worthy of your calling, for you have been called by God. Always be humble and gentle. Be patient with each other, making allowance for each other's faults because of your love. Make every effort to keep yourselves united in the Spirit, binding yourselves together with peace. For there is one body and one Spirit, just as you have been called to one glorious hope for the future. There is one Lord, one faith, one baptism, one God and Father of all,who is over all, in all, and living through all."

There is one Lord, one Faith, one Baptism, one God, and Father of all who is over all, in all, and living through all.

This scripture speaks about the unification of yourself with God; mind, body, and spirit.

God chose us for this unification.

As God's chosen people we are called to live according to God's Word. To go deeper God gets specific on how to live in such a manner.

We should never think of ourselves as better than anyone else. There is no "Better" in relation from one person to another. God created us all uniquely, intentionally with no real similarities that would cause us to be just a like or for us to look at one another and judge based on who we are.

That is not God's choice for us. We were all uniquely made for something specific, something only we can do.

No two people will walk the same path and or experience life the same.

Yes, the rules are the same but the intended outcomes are set to be different.

God instructs us with simple instruction that encompass so much of our attitude and behavior toward others like:

- Be kind and Patient
- Love each other
- Don't be so quick to get upset or angry with one another

In all things do your best to let the Holy Spirit be your guide. It keeps us on the right track, God's planned path.

God wants us to operate from a place of believing:

- We are one body of believers
- Being led by one spirit
- Believing in on God

All receiving and trusting in the same God!!!

He created us all

He is all of our Father

He is over all

He is in all

Living through is all!!!!

Make sure your relationship with God is the most important one. You identity, your path, you process, your life, your future, your success is all tied to that primary relationship is impenetrable and absolutely necessary.

4:14 "Then we will no longer be immature like children. We will not be tossed and blown about by every wind of new teaching. We will not be influenced when people try to trick us with lies so clever they sound like the truth.

Once you make the major choice to believe and follow, a spiritual maturing will manifest outward and in the natural. Once you are guided and led by the Word of God and the leading of the Holy Spirit, the devil, his soldiers or their attempts will not easily sway you.

The world, social media, and anybody teaching contrary to the word of God will always be catalyst for the devil to influence with tricks, charm, and plenty of cleverness and tied into the lies told and or shown.

Satan is a false perpetrator of truth.... The Father of Lies!

4:25 "So stop telling lies. Let us tell our neighbors the truth, for we are all parts of the same body.

As believers in the same God, we must not indulge in lies, the truth must be 1st nature no options for the other.

We are one body, no point in lying to ourselves.

4:26 "And don't sin by letting anger control you. Don't let the sun go down while you are still angry for anger gives a foothold to the devil.

Acting out of anger is a seed from our sinful nature, and will cause you to sin doing thing God would not be please with.

God urges us about holding on to it and it absolutely not good to go to sleep with it because it festers causing discomfort and disconnect between you and the creator. When you are angry, you are not hearing clearly from God and if you are you are not listening or adhering to him and you are giving a person, situation, or circumstance more control over you, your thoughts, and behavior than God.

Anger and acting out of anger gives the devil an entry way to you, your thoughts, and behavior giving him an opportunity to sow bad seed whose manifestation will no doubt be bad.

Bad seed produce bad trees, which produce bad fruit.

Beware of the type of soil you are.

Guard you heart, mind and soul!!!

Block the Bad Seed.

4:31-32 "Get rid of all bitterness, rage, anger, harsh words, and slander, as well as all types of evil behavior. Instead, be kind to each other, tenderhearted, forgiving one another, just as God through Christ has forgiven you."

Don't hold on to things that aren't of God. It can manifest in ways that would be unexpected and unwanted.

Forgive, Love, Move On, Move Forward

Trust God to protect you, sometimes that means having to learn hard lessons through unwarranted and undesirable experiences.

God, His Word, the Holy Spirit are the major things you are supposed to take hold of. This hold has no limits or expiration it is forever and guaranteed.

5:1-7 (Living in the Light) "Imitate God, therefore, in everything you do, because you are his dear children. Live a life filled with love, following the example of Christ. He loved us and offered himself as a sacrifice for us, a pleasing aroma to God. Let there be no sexual immorality, impurity, or greed among you. Such sins have no place among God's people. Obscene stories, foolish talk, and coarse jokes—these are not for you. Instead, let there be thankfulness to God. You can be sure that no immoral, impure, or greedy person will inherit the Kingdom of Christ and of God. For a greedy person is an idolater, worshiping the things of this world. Do not be fooled by those who try to excuse these sins, for the anger of God will fall on all who disobey him. Don't participate in the things these people do."

God's chosen people must be ok with being different from the norm, different, non-conforming.

The scripture says imitate because God knows we can never be just like him but following his lead and doing things his way will lead us to the promise of God and the life he intended each of us to have.

Seek God 1st in all things to ensure that all things are properly aligned.

His way leads to a life filled with love.

God loves us unconditionally and gave the ultimate sacrifice he made for us should alone give us such a sense of overwhelming acceptance and love that make you want to live a life that is pleasing to God, your Father and creator.

He wants us to live a life of pureness, free of greed, and not lead by our flesh. Sins that go against these things don't belong in us.

We must even mature further to not indulge in talks, or scenarios, or even jokes that celebrate who the devil is or what he is selling or representing.

We must not entertain the devil or celebrate who he is through our behavior or daily living.

Must live a life of thankfulness carrying an attitude of gratitude to God.

No one who knowingly choosing to live for Satan will inherit the Kingdom of God.

Greed is one we should definitely beware of and stay away from. Greed means you will do anything to quench this thirst. You can't have a no matter what attitude with anything accept for God, and you walk.

Greed is about loving things of this world.

Beware of those who justify their sins instead of repenting and turning from them.

The anger of God will follow those who disobey him. Refrain from things that displease God!!!

Philippians

2:2-8 "Then make me truly happy by agreeing wholeheartedly with each other, loving one another, and working together with one mind and purpose. Don't be selfish; don't try to impress others. Be humble, thinking of others as better than yourselves. Don't look out only for your own interests, but take an interest in others, too. You must have the same attitude that Christ Jesus had. Though he was God, he did not think of equality with God as something to cling to. Instead, he gave up his divine privileges; he took the humble position of a slave and was born as a human being. When he appeared in human form, he humbled himself in obedience to God and died a criminal's death on a cross.

As God's chosen people in our day to day lives and how we operate should be pleasing to God. If we are led by one spirit, we should be in agreement with little to no discord, loving each other freely not because of common thoughts but because of a common creator, working together serving individual purposes fulfilling God's plan.

We are to be selfless only seeking to impress and please God.

Be humble, only seeing yourself and others as God does. Come to a true understanding that taking an interest in others is necessary as we take an interest in our self.

We must adapt and take hold and maintain an attitude that of which is life Jesus Christ.

3:18-19 "For I have told you often before, and I say it again with tears in my eyes, that there are many whose conduct shows they are really enemies of the cross of Christ. They are headed for destruction. Their god is their appetite, they brag about shameful things, and they think only about this life here on earth.

Another urging scripture warning us yet again about the conduct of those who we can only believe are true enemies of the Cross of Christ. The behavior reveals a path of destruction and the appetite of the one they serve. These people we are very familiar with because they actually brag about what they do, their intent, and motivation.

A clear sign is also their major concern is only for their life here on earth and not their place in the Kingdom of God.

4:8-9 "And now, dear brothers and sisters, one final thing. Fix your thoughts on what is true, and honorable, and right, and pure, and lovely, and admirable. Think about things that are excellent and worthy of praise. Keep putting into practice all you learned and received from me—everything you heard from me and saw me doing. Then the God of peace will be with you."

This scripture is a great reminder that our thoughts will cause the manifestation of these thing in our life.

If our thoughts are based on:

- Truth
- What is honorable
- What is right
- What is pure
- What is lovely
- What is admirable

It will manifest as living a life of

- Truth, with honor, in righteousness, pure in heart, rich in love, and a life to be admired.

Thinking about things that are excellent and praise worthy, we shall experience thing of excellence and things that we can give God the highest praise and Glory for.

Colossians

2:8-9 "Don't let anyone capture you with empty philosophies and high-sounding nonsense that come from human thinking and from the spiritual powers of this world, rather than from Christ. For in Christ lives all the fullness of God in a human body.

Don't get caught up in verbal fluff meant to contradict and discredit the Word of God.

The Word of God is the foundation of all things, or at least it should be.

Human thinking fights to rationalize God and the Word of God.

Human thinking requires no faith.....

All thinking should be derived from God and God alone.

There are no original thoughts, they either come from God or the Devil.

There is no gray area.

Know from where your thoughts flow from don't be scared to challenge your own thoughts against the world. This will allow you to operate more confidently and freely on God's behalf.

3:5-10 "So put to death the sinful, earthly things lurking within you. Have nothing to do with sexual immorality, impurity, lust, and evil desires. Don't be greedy, for a greedy person is an idolater, worshiping the things of this world. Because of these sins, the anger of God is coming. You used to do these things when your life was still part of this world. But now is the time to get rid of anger, rage, malicious behavior, slander, and dirty language. Don't lie to each other, for you have stripped off your old sinful nature and all its wicked deeds. Put on your new nature, and be renewed as you learn to know your Creator and become like him."

This scripture instructs us further to turn from our sinful nature and the sinful things we do here on earth.

Turn away from(God is specific)

- Sexual immorality
- Impurity
- Lust
- Evil Desires

Avoid being greedy because greed causes us to worship things of this world.

These wrongs anger God and you will see consequences. Yes, he will forgive, BUT we do not escape our consequences. Consequences and punishment are to correct us, and to ensure the lesson is learned. God is not cruel; He corrects us out of Love.

What would be the lesson if all he did was forgive? We are called to do the right thing based on the choices presented. God gave us the freedom to choose, he even warns us to help us make the correct decision. Often times we allow our flesh, emotions, and other things to mislead us and distract us from God's plan and the correct choice.

We must stay focused on the things of God, so when the things not of God approach we are on HIGH ALERT and ready to deflect.

Be careful to not let anything have more control over you than God.

Once we chose God we are to clean ourselves of thing that keep us tied to the old you.

Release ourselves of anger, rage, malicious behavior, slander, and dirty language.

Avoid lying................Period!!!

Do not lie to yourself or others. Lies are bad seed!

Embrace you new ways of living, constantly renewing your mind, body, and spirit as you study the Word and following the leading of the Holy Spirit.

Become like Christ

See things A God does

Believe as God does

Think as God does

Seek Him 1st in all things!!!

2 Thessalonians

2:2-3 "Don't be so easily shaken or alarmed by those who say that the day of the Lord has already begun. Don't believe them, even if they claim to have had a spiritual vision, a revelation, or a letter supposedly from us. Don't be fooled by what they say. For that day will not come until there is a great rebellion against God and the man of lawlessness is revealed—the one who brings destruction.

Beware of those that claim to know what God himself has yet to reveal.

Don't be afraid to check the spiritual connection of those who say they operate on behalf of God. Their life will be evident of what they believe.

Remember good fruit comes from good trees.

2:9-12 "This man will come to do the work of Satan with counterfeit power and signs and miracles. He will use every kind of evil deception to fool those on their way to destruction, because they refuse to love and accept the truth that would save them. So God will cause them to be greatly deceived, and they will believe these lies. Then they will be condemned for enjoying evil rather than believing the truth."

This scripture refers to the man of lawlessness. He is a soldier for Satan dealing in counterfeit powers, signs, and miracles. He will be a master of all evil and deception with the intent to fool those headed for destruction.

Those headed for destruction refuse to love and accept the truth, but it is love and acceptance of God's Word that will ultimately save them.

Because they refuse to love or accept God's truth, God will cause them to be deceived and they will believe the devil and all his lies.

These people will be punished for partaking and enjoying evil instead of operating in truth.

1 Timothy

2:14 "And it was not Adam who was deceived by Satan. The woman was deceived, and sin was the result."

This scripture brings clarity about who was actually deceived and how the deception led to Sin.

Deception will always be sinful or lead to sin. Deception is a tool and or weapon of Satan.

4:1 "Now the Holy Spirit tells us clearly that in the last times some will turn away from the true faith; they will follow deceptive spirits and teachings that come from demons."

This is a scripture about an urging or leading from the Holy Spirit stating that as signs of our last days people will turn from true faith and follow Satan and his evil spirits.

2 Timothy

3:12-13 "Yes, and everyone who wants to live a godly life in Christ Jesus will suffer persecution. But evil people and impostors will flourish. They will deceive others and will themselves be deceived."

This scripture often times trip people up. Don't be deceived by what you see!!!

People who chose to lead a Godly life following the example of Jesus Christ will suffer persecution.

People who knowingly choose wrong and follow evil will somehow flourish.

This is a deception; people who are led by Satan may believe they are flourishing or progressing but things of Satan don't last.

Don't be deceived by what you SEE!!!!!!

People who progress by way of Satan will experience a downfall like no other.

No God comes from Satan or his seeds!!!!

Don't be misled by those who are not being led by God.

4:3-4 "For a time is coming when people will no longer listen to sound and wholesome teaching. They will follow their own desires and will look for teachers who will tell them whatever their itching ears want to hear. They will reject the truth and chase after myths.

This scripture is a clear depiction of this world, society, social media, and government vs God, the supernatural, and the kingdom of God.

This covers a time which is more like the present where people are listening to and being misled by their own desires that stem from what the world offers instead of what God promises.

People are constantly searching for validation of who they either think they want to be or who the world says they are or can be vs Who God says you are, can be and ultimately who God created you to be.

This world misled us and we make bad choices based on this worlds deception and unfounded promises of more and better.

Know the Truth....

Operate from a place of truth!

Don't chase things of this world and the things this world says is yours or that you can have.

Chase after the promises of God.

Pursue God and his righteousness

Seek to please God in your day-to-day living

Everything must line up with the Word if it doesn't disregard, rebuke, turn away, and deflect.

Beware of people who validate wrong, bad, evil behavior or actions.

Hebrews

13:1-3 "Keep on loving each other as brothers and sisters. Don't forget to show hospitality to strangers, for some who have done this have entertained angels without realizing it! Remember those in prison, as if you were there yourself. Remember also those being mistreated, as if you felt their pain in your own bodies."

Remember those in prison, as if you were there yourself. Remember also those being mistreated as if you felt their pain in your own bodies.

Again a scripture reiterating the importance of Love.

Reminds us to be kind to all no matter the relation, and in doing so you never know the great seeds you are sowing and to whom you have been a visible example of God for.

Don't forget those in prison this isn't only in regard to physical prison; it could also be mental prison, or spiritual prison. Physical prison could be in reference to jail, lock up, county, or penitentiary.

But there are also physical limitations that prevent us from living freely according to the Word of God and his plan for each of our lives.

Mental prison has to do with mental limitations preventing us from acting and being according to Gods Word. Our actions flow from our mental or thoughts.

Spiritual prison is any spiritual limitations that prevent you from fully following the Word of God, heart, mind, body, and soul, to be free to live as God planned with the ultimate goal being to become who God created you to be.

This scripture wants you to have empathy for those imprisoned or in pain.

Be compassionate.

13:18 "Pray for us, for our conscience is clear and we want to live honorably in everything we do."

Pray for one another as spiritual leaders living according to God's purpose and plan living with a clear conscience or right spirit.

Live, behave, act in an honorable manor in all things.

James

1:19-20 "Understand this, my dear brothers and sisters: You must all be quick to listen, slow to speak, and slow to get angry. Human anger does not produce the righteousness God desires."

This scripture is one most of us need to work on. Most of us are quick to not listen quickly to speak, and even quicker to get angry. All these things are harmful to our walk.

We must learn to listen actively!

Process all information completely before speaking. Seek God about the information, and speak according to God's Word, and avoid getting angry all together.

Speaking with anger or from an angry place will lead you to sowing bad seed in your life and or someone else.

Human anger doesn't lead us to righteousness.

Righteousness is God's desire for us.

1:22-27 "But don't just listen to God's word. You must do what it says. Otherwise, you are only fooling yourselves. For if you listen to the word and don't obey, it is like glancing at your face in a mirror. You see yourself, walk away, and forget what you look like. But if you look carefully into the perfect law that sets you free, and if you do what it says and don't forget what you heard, then God will bless you for doing it. If you claim to be religious but don't control your tongue, you are fooling yourself, and your religion is worthless. Pure and genuine religion in the sight of God the Father means caring for orphans and widows in their distress and refusing to let the world corrupt you."

God's Word is not just to be read or just listened to, you must do and obey and allow it to be your guide for your day to day living.

To hear the Word or read the Word and not take heed you are only fooling yourself. Your heart isn't in it and your life can't be positively impacted.

The Word of God will set you free and when you follow and obey, God WILL bless you for doing so.

You won't regret obeying God and following the leading of the Holy Spirit.

If you are claiming to be spiritual your behavior must be consistent with that, you must practice self-control, control your words, actions, and thoughts.

Don't fool or lie to yourself.

Being pure and genuine in God eyes shows your spiritual nature, and it shows up in your intersection with others, how you care for those God brings across your path, and the refusal to let the world corrupt you, your life, mind, or future.

Don't be misled by this world it will corrupt your path and efforts causing delays and unnecessary diversions.

2:8 "Yes indeed, it is good when you obey the royal law as found in the scriptures: Love your neighbor as yourself.

Obeying God is the most rewarding thing you will ever do. When you obey God, you don't have to look over your shoulders to see what is coming. You can trust what is to come because your steps are ordered and when you take your ordered steps you are in the will of God which is an ultimate goal.

This scripture instructs us to love others as we love ourselves. This forms a major problem/issue since most people lack self-love. If you don't love yourself, you can't truly love anyone else.

Self-love helps you love others as well as shows people how to love you as well.

4:1 "What is causing the quarrels and fights among you? Don't they come from the evil desires at war within you?"

This scripture speaks of why people fight others or even themselves.

Fighting is an action that stems from anger and anger is a seed from Satan.

This seed feeds the evil desires within a person and causes them to act in disapproving ways based on God's Word.

4:11-12 "Don't speak evil against each other, dear brothers and sisters. If you criticize and judge each other, then you are criticizing and judging God's law. But your job is to obey the law, not to judge whether it applies to you. God alone, who gave the law, is the Judge. He alone has the power to save or to destroy. So what right do you have to judge your neighbor?"

God is so direct and so literal sometimes in his instructions and urgings.

In this scripture God speaks again about evil and speaking evil against others.

God doesn't like for us to criticize each other or judge each, because no one is perfect and God doesn't require perfection.

Our job in God's eyes is to obey his Word, and never judge others for who or what they do.

God needs no help as judge. God alone can save or destroy.

We should never act as if we are God.

1Peter

2:1-3 "So get rid of all evil behavior. Be done with all deceit, hypocrisy, jealousy, and all unkind speech. Like newborn babies, you must crave pure spiritual milk so that you will grow into a full experience of salvation. Cry out for this nourishment, now that you have had a taste of the Lord's kindness.

Oh yeah these are ones.... Must Do!!!!

Turn from any and all things that serve the okan of the devil. Have self control doing and saying things that please God ONLY.

Avoid deceit of any kind.

Don't tell others to stop doing wrong when you are doing wrong.

Show them how to live right. Be a person of action.

Be grateful for who God created YOU to be.

Be grateful for all God has done for YOU.

Don't be jealous of others in any regard.

Speak only kind words which is Good SEED.

Beware of sowing bad seed through your speaking. Be mindful of how you use your Words.

4:7 "The end of the world is coming soon. Therefore, be earnest and disciplined in your prayers."

One of our greatest weapons and forms of communication is Prayer.

As this world continues to head for a projected end, be mindful, be serious-minded, and discipline in your prayer life.

Prayer life is necessary in your process of becoming who God created you to be. It is also the tool we use to seek God in all things, and to ensure that our relationship with God is 1st and intact.

1John

1:8 "If we claim we have no sin, we are only fooling ourselves and not living in the truth."

This scripture lets us know no one is perfect and it shouldn't be expected or demanded. Any one believing they are perfect or can be perfect is wrong and can't live in truth and be free.

2:16 "For the world offers only a craving for physical pleasure, a craving for everything we see, and pride in our achievements and possessions. These are not from the Father, but are from this world."

The world sets out to appeal to our physical senses, and seek to lead us based on what appeals to our sight, smell, taste, hearing, and touch.

This world serves our flesh and the desires of the flesh.

This world wants us to celebrate things it wants us to believe we achieved without God and things we obtained or received without God.

But there is no true success without God and the possessions we are to value are those God has given or plan to give.

The things of this world are not from God.

4:1 "Dear friends, do not believe everyone who claims to speak by the Spirit. You must test them to see if the spirit they have comes from God. For there are many false prophets in the world."

Everyone who says they are spirit led are not actually lead by the spirit but by Satan and his evil spirit.

You must test all spirits before you follow.

If the spirit is from God, he will lead to God, his plan, and purpose.

5:19 "We know that we are children of God and that the world around us is under the control of the evil one."

Scripture that states an operating truth. We should operate as God's children and be ware and don't fall under the control of Satan.

Revelations

12:9 "This great dragon—the ancient serpent called the devil, or Satan, the one deceiving the whole world—was thrown down to the earth with all his angels."

Satan was once an angel who has been thrown down to earth and his plan is to deceive the whole world.

Beware of all form of deception, they are the devils fools!

13:13-14 "He did astounding miracles, even making fire flash down to earth from the sky while everyone was watching. And with all the miracles he was allowed to perform on behalf of the first beast, he deceived all the people who belong to this world. He ordered the people to make a great statue of the first beast, who was fatally wounded and then came back to life."

This painted a visual of just how slick and deceptive the devil is. He has the ability to make you believe you are being blessed by recurring perceived miracles.

His goal is to deceive all people of this world, which is why you must choose to be in this world but not of this world. Reside in the supernatural where God reigns supreme.

Be in the world but not of it. Choose to follow God's law and the leading of the Holy Spirit and we will experience the supernatural.

This world is not for us!

This world doesn't have your best interest at heart, only God our creator, our most perfect parent does.

This world and those that run it are self-serving.

Make your choice and know that your life and the results of your daily living will reflect what you truly believe.

We receive according to what we believe!

21:8 "But cowards, unbelievers, the corrupt, murderers, the immoral, those who practice witchcraft, idol worshipers, and all liars—their fate is in the fiery lake of burning sulfur. This is the second death."

Avoid falling into any of these categories for their fate has already been determined.

These people aren't serving God or their Purpose!

Sign of Self Sabotage/Self Deception

1. Always blaming someone else for the bad, taking no accountability for your actions or choice in the matter.

2. Allowing others to impact and affect you more than God.

3. You don't see yourself as God sees you.

4. You don't try cause you are scared to fail

5. You don't surround yourself with people who allows and encourages growth.

How Satan uses people

Satan is intentional in his actions, he has soldiers and he recruits non-believers or those that struggle with their beliefs.

Most don't willingly play along but when you are not living according to the Word, being led by the Holy Spirit, and seeking God 1st in all things you open yourself up to be used by Satan.

Seek to please God in all things, align everything you do, say and believe with the Word of God.

Also pray for discernment so you can know when satan is trying to get to you and how.

Discernment is necessary as you walk through this life, path, and journey.

The Distractions

The devil will attempt to distract us, so that we cant become who God created us to be.

He will use things that appeal to our flesh emotions, and or worldly desires to keep us off track and block our efforts to getting on track.

We must get, stay, and remain focused on the things of God.

Seeking him 1st in all things keep us aligned with God's will for our lives, giving the devil little to no chance to interrupt or disrupt our process.

We must fully embrace the process of becoming who God created us to be, and to do that we can't entertain the devil, his soldiers, or attempts.

Discernment will allow us to see satan coming which we can rebuke, and put on the full armor of God and use our weapons of spiritual warfare.

Your Worth and Value

You are a Child of God!

You were created by the most high for a greater purpose, greater than ourselves.

You were created for a specific purpose to play a specific part in his plan for the Kingdom of God.

We are all called!!!

This world tries to defines is using a variety of determining factors that are actually irrelevant to our worth.

Our worth was defined when God sacrificed his son for us.

We are priceless!!! But we often sale ourselves short cause we believe the lies of this world.

You are a uniquely made masterpiece created by The Master of Creation.

Don't allow this world to devalue because they see no value in the God who created you.

Don't allow those who see no value in themselves, make you feel worthless.

Your value and worth is linked to the one who created you and know your ending before your beginning.

Don't believe that your value and worth is based on your occupation, salary, or life achievements.

Your worth is tied to God and the sacrifice he made so that we can have life

A life free of sin, sickness, and lack...etc

A life full of promise!!!

Chapter 7
Playing the Role God places you in

Child of God

Who are you?

How do you define who you are?

Understand the answers to these questions will not answer the prior questions:

- What is you name
- Who are your parents
- Where are you from

You are a Child of God

Initially we are all God's children

God picked your parents so that you would get certain characteristic from them that help mold you.

You are not to become mini versions of your parents.

That is a common mistake among parents they try and raise their children according to who they are instead of according to who God says their children will be.

No two people are to be exactly alike.

Value the things about yourself that make you different. Quit trying to blend in.

Ask God who your children are and ask God to lead you in your role as a parent, so that you child will also be in the Will of God and on track to become who God created them to become who God created them to be.

Being a child of God has its own defining character traits.

How you behave, speak, live, and interact with others will let others know who you are.

We are all defined by these things!!!

But please don't take on the labels this world tries to put on you as they only serve to control, confine, and limit what God has put no limits on.

Remember you can do all things through Christ who strengthens you.

Wear the label Child of God proudly, understand what comes along with that:

- Unconditional love
- Forgiveness
- No lack
- Abundance
- Free from pain
- Free from sickness
- Fruitful living
- Strength in times of weakness
- Supernatural Favor
- Supernatural Blessings
- Ordered Steps
- Freedom to be all God created you to be
- Freedom to receive all the promises of God

- Freedom to do all he created you to do

- Freedom to say all the things he created you to say

Learn and know who your creator is, this will give you great insight into who you are. We often times look to family or our birth parents for similarities or character traits that feel familiar or comfortable.

You need to use the Word of God as your guide and compass.

Everyone's journey is personal even our parents. Being your parent or guardian is one aspect of who they are and their journey only intercepts with your. Often times because of the relationship we tend to personalize our parents choices and allowing who they are, what they do, and how they decide to live to have a bigger effect on who we are and who we are to become than God.

Learn to tap into your Heavenly Father to get the necessary guidance and insight on how to become who God created you to be.

And this starts with knowing you are a Child of God.

1. Galatians 3:26 – "For you are all sons of God through faith in Christ Jesus."

2. 2 Corinthians 6:18 – "And I will be a father to you, and you shall be sons and daughters to me," Says the Lord Almighty."

3. Romans 8:14 – "For all who are being led by the Spirit of God, these are sons of God.

4. Galatians 4:7 – "therefore you are no longer a slave, but a son, and if a son then an heir through God"

5. Matthew 19:14 – "But Jesus said, Let the children alone, and do not hinder them from coming to me; for the kingdom of heaven belongs to such as these."

6. Psalms 127:3 – "Behold, children are a gift of the Lord, the fruit of the womb is a reward."

7. Isaiah 44:3 – "For I will pour out water to quench your thirst and to irrigate your parched fields. And I will pour out my Spirit on your descendants, and my blessing on your children."

8. John 1:12 – "But as many as received Him, to them H egave the right to become children of God, even to those who believe in his name.

9. 1 John 3:10 – "By this the children of God and the children of the devil are obvious; anyone who does not practice righteousness is not of God, nor the one who does not love his brother."

10. Isaiah 54:13 – "All your sons will be taught of the Lord; And the well-being of your sons will be great.

11. Isaiah 8:18 – "Behold, I and the children whom the Lord has given me are for the signs and wonders in Israel from the Lord of Host, who dwells on Mt Zion"

12. Genesis 1:27 – "God created man in His own image in the image of God He created Him, male and Female. He created them."

Gifts from God

- Wisdom
- Understanding
- Counsel
- Fortitude
- Knowledge
- Piety
- Fear of the Lord

The Natural vs The Supernatural

The natural refers to the worldly realm.

The supernatural refers to the spiritual realm.

The supernatural is the greater of the two.

The natural serves your flesh and draws us away from the supernatural.

The natural is lived through our physical senses.

The supernatural is based on God, His Word, and His Will for the kingdom of God and we are led according to revelations from God through the leading of the Holy Spirit.

There is life and peace in the supernatural.

There death in the natural.

The natural is where we reside when not attached to God.

The natural is where you reside when God, his Word, or his Will is not leading us. Which shows that being in the natural isn't Gods Will..... Period.

God doesn't want us to conform to this world.

1 John 2:15-17 (Do not Love this World)

"Do not love this world nor the things it offers you, for when you love the world, you do not have the love of the Father in you. For the world offers only a craving for physical pleasure, a craving for everything we see, and pride in our achievements and possessions. These arc not from the Father, but are from this world. And this world is fading away, along with everything that people crave. But anyone who does what pleases God will live forever."

The natural is where non-believers reside. The world tells them who they can be (labels), How to achieve it (control), the height one can reach by living according to the world (confine).

The supernatural is where the believers reside. People who have chosen to live a life led by God, obeying God, and believing in who God says you are.

In the supernatural is where the Word has Power and your Faith can and will move mountains.

In the supernatural is where we experience God's goodness, unconditional love, and forgiveness.

What you believe and how you live will be a tell tell sign of where you reside.

Remember: *We receive according to what we believe.*

We can't obey the world and expect to receive from God.

When we obey God and follow his leading, we will exceed the limits this world has tried to put on us.

The supernatural will far exceed our imagination.

Ephesians 3:20 "Now all glory to God, who is able, through his mighty power at work within us, to accomplish infinitely more than we might ask or think."

In the supernatural the Word of God reigns supreme.

In order to receive from God you must reside in the supernatural.

Most people in the natural realm receive grace and mercy, which is what God, gives us when we are not where we should be spiritually.

The Impact

Your life; every area of your life should be impacted by God, His Word, and His Will for your life, and his will for the Kingdom.

5 Central Areas of to focus on

- Spiritual
- Education
- Occupation
- Physical
- Mental

Seeking God in these 5 areas consistently will change, correct, and improve your life.

If you allow God, his Word, and his Will to guide you in all things and allow the Holy Spirit to lead you according to the same Word and Will.

You can confidently walk and speak knowing you are covered because you are in the Will of God.

You can step confidently without worry of what is to come, because what follows obedience is blessing, miracles, a great many rewards.

Allow God to impact you in a way that when people see or hear you they know God exist.

Once we allow God to fully impact t us completely wc will experience:

- Healing
- Being Made Whole
- Assurance
- Peace
- Unspeakable Joy

Once we receive these things we must faithfully walk in those thing, claiming nothing that contradicts these valued God experiences.

Don't allow Satan to devalue the things God gives us to better us.

God isn't wasteful.

He intended to impact our lives in a way that we change the world and lead others to him.

We were created to be impacted and to be an impact.

In your uniqueness allow God to use you for a purpose greater than yourself.

Allowing God to use you to impact others will improve your quality of life!!!

Also you will find that you get to experience more God moments when you are a willing vessel.

The more God experiences you are exposed to the more your faith will increase.

When you allow yourself to be fully impacted by God your Faith will increase.

You will be completely sold out for the Lord.

Key: Never let anything or anyone have more control over you than God and the Word of God.

Be impenetrable.

The Purpose – Part of the Plan

1 Corithians 12:12-27 "Just as a body, though one, has many parts, but all its many parts form one body, so it is with Christ. For we were all baptized by[c] one Spirit so as to form one body—whether Jews or Gentiles, slave or free—and we were all given the one Spirit to drink. Even so the body is not made up of one part but of many. Now if the foot should say, "Because I am not a hand, I do not belong to the body," it would not for that reason stop being part of the body. And if the ear should say, "Because I am not an eye, I do not belong to the body," it would not for that reason stop being part of the body. If the whole body were an eye, where would the sense of hearing be? If the whole body were an ear, where would the sense of smell

be? But in fact God has placed the parts in the body, every one of them, just as he wanted them to be. If they were all one part, where would the body be? As it is, there are many parts, but one body.The eye cannot say to the hand, "I don't need you!" And the head cannot say to the feet, "I don't need you!" On the contrary, those parts of the body that seem to be weaker are indispensable,and the parts that we think are less honorable we treat with special honor. And the parts that are unpresentable are treated with special modesty, while our presentable parts need no special treatment. But God has put the body together, giving greater honor to the parts that lacked it, so that there should be no division in the body, but that its parts should have equal concern for each other. If one part suffers, every part suffers with it; if one part is honored, every part rejoices with it. Now you are the body of Christ, and each one of you is a part of it."

This scripture describes how God sees us and how he intended us to live in this world and how we are to experience and encounter each other.

We as children are as one body operating for the same kingdom, all being called to serve and or play a different role.

In this one body we are all lead by one Spirit, The Holy Spirit.

We were all created to receive the same spirit led to live our own lives positively impacting those God planned to cross or intercept our God ordained paths.

The body included all believers, all of God's children. All of us was created for a specific purpose to serve within the body!

Being a child of God and your belief is what makes you a part of the body.

No member of the body should assume that because they aren't a part because of the roles the other members play. We are necessary and no less or more important than the other. We are significant and no less important. Every role has a purpose in the Kingdom of God.

Play the role God has called you to, waste no time, energy, or effort on trying to be any other member or part. No need to over compensate for where others may or may not fulfill their own purpose, that is Gods arena and he is all knowing and all powerful.

Every part is purposed to ensure the existence and fulfillment of God's Plan for us and his kingdom.

God is and was intentional on who does what, why they do it, when to do it, and how.

Once everyone is playing the role God gave them according to the rules he laid out in the Bible these is a cohesiveness that leads to progress, and a great spiritual evolution as God pre-planned.

Remember: Jeremiah 1:5 "Before I formed you in the womb I knew you, before you were born I set you apart; I appointed you as a prophet to the nations."

Romans 2:11 "For God does not show favoritism"

God is no respecter of persons. What he will do for one he will do for another.

Our cohesiveness forms the Body, without the body we are simply parts with no purpose.

In God's eyes, it is the weaker parts of the body that he gives a greater honor, in our weakness is where God strength can find a place, allowing for no room for division in the body.

God wants us to have some care for each other as he has for us.

He wants his to see ourselves as he sees us.

He wants us to see others the way he sees them.

What affects one part of the body will affect the whole body, both pain and suffering and honor and rejoicing.

Reflect on Jesus; and how he dying on the cross was for our sins.

We are all part of one body but individually we are children of God called to impact the world as one Body!!!

Chapter 8

The Difficulties and Pitfalls

Galatians 5:16-26 "But I say, walk by the Spirit, and you will not gratify the desires of the flesh. For the desires of the flesh are against the Spirit, and the desires of the Spirit are against the flesh, for these are opposed to each other, to keep you from doing the things you want to do. But if you are led by the Spirit, you are not under the law. Now the works of the flesh are evident:

- sexual immorality,
- impurity,
- sensuality,
- idolatry,
- sorcery,
- enmity,
- strife,
- jealousy,
- fits of anger,
- rivalries,
- dissensions,
- divisions
- envy,
- drunkenness,

- orgies,
- things like these

I warn you, as I warned you before, that those who do such things will not inherit the kingdom of God. But the fruit of the Spirit is:

- love,

- joy,

- peace,

- patience,

- kindness,

- goodness,

- faithfulness,

- gentleness,

- self-control;

- against such things there is no law.

And those who belong to Christ Jesus have crucified the flesh with its passions and desires. If we live by the Spirit, let us also keep in step with the Spirit. Let us not become conceited, provoking one another, envying one another."

One of our major pitfalls or things that causes a challenge to our walk and process of becoming who od created us to be is our flesh.

Our flesh if not spirit led will lead us astray.

Our flesh is what the devil seeks to use against us to throw us off course and to negatively affect others and their walk as well.

Be unavailable to Satan and his soldiers.

This scripture is one every believer should know, read, study, and meditate on as it is guidance and instruction that leads you and keeps you on the correct path and in God's Will.

Paul instructs us in these verses to walk by the spirit of God and in doing so we will not be misled by our flesh.

The desires that are set to please our flesh are not from the Spirit.

Flesh and Spirit are in opposition until your flesh submits to your spirit man. That can't happen until your spirit man is stronger than your flesh. This is evident in a spirit led life.

Flesh is selfish and self-serving.

Spirit is God-Minded and God Led.

Lack of Knowledge

Hosea 4:6 "My people are destroyed because they have not learned. You were not willing to learn. So I am not willing to have you be My religious leader. Since you have forgotten the Law of your God, I also will forget your children."

Clearly in this scripture God is concerned about our destruction. Destruction comes if we don't have and live by the knowledge of God, and the knowledge of the Word of God.

We are supposed to operate from this knowledge allowing God's Word and Will to be what is guiding us in our day to day living.

If you choose to not live according to this knowledge and choose rejecting God's instruction on how to live, be, and act, he too can reject you.

Don't forget God's Word, So that he doesn't forget you!

Be mindful of God, and who he is to us!!!

The Great I am

Alpha and Omega

Isaiah 5:13 "So My people are taken away to strange lands because they have not been wise. Their men of honor are dying because they are hungry. Their people are dried up because they are thirsty."

Due to us not seeking and choosing God's knowledge as our own it makes us available to Satan to captivate and enslave for his plan and purpose.

No knowledge will lead to lack and an unquenchable thirst.

Romans 10:17 "So then, faith comes to us by hearing the Good News. And the Good News comes by someone preaching it."

The Word of God is knowledge, hearing the Word of God and living by his Word and Will, will lead you to receiving and living by Faith.

God instructs us to read, learn, hear, and meditate on his Word.

John 8:32 "You will know the truth and the truth will make you free."

Believing and living according to the Word of God leads us to freedom.

Knowing the truth which is the infallible Word of God; will lead us in living a life of truth.

There is freedom in living according to God's Word.

Ephesians 1:17-21 "I pray that the great God and Father of our Lord Jesus Christ may give you the wisdom of His Spirit. Then you will be able to understand the secrets about Him as you know Him better. I pray that your hearts will be able to understand. I pray that you will know about the hope given by God's call. I pray that you will see how great the things are that He has promised to those who belong to Him. I pray that you will know how great His power is for those who have put their trust in Him. It is the same power that raised Christ from the dead. This same power put Christ at God's right side in heaven. 21 This place was given to Christ. It is much greater than any king or leader can have. No one else can have this place of honor and power. No one in this world or in the world to come can have such honor and power. God has put all things under Christ's power and has made Him to be the head leader over all things of the church. The church is the body of Christ. It is filled by Him Who fills all things everywhere with Himself."

God gives us his wisdom and revelation based on the knowledge in the Word of God.

The wisdom and knowledge enlighten our heart and leads us to having hope in life and all that you do.

The wisdom and knowledge lead us to the riches of his inheritance in the saints.

We also get to experience God's immeasurable greatness of his power toward all believers; and this will be according to God's great might that was shown when raising Jesus from the dead and sitting him in his rightful place.

Where God resides and his laws are above all other rules, authority, power, and dominions.

For all times there will never be a name above God.

God establishes all things under him and his fullness fills all things.

Proverbs 1:3-8 "They help you learn about the ways of wisdom and what is right and fair. They give wisdom to the child-like, and much learning and wisdom to those who are young. A wise man will hear and grow in learning. A man of understanding will become able to understand a saying and a picture-story, the words of the wise and what they mean. The fear of the Lord is the beginning of much learning. Fools hate wisdom and teaching. Hear your father's teaching, my son, and do not turn away from your mother's teaching."

The book of Proverbs was written to teach God's children how to live disciplined and successful lives.

It leads us to what is right, just, and fair according to the Word of God.

Proverbs keep it simple, full of knowledge and teaches discernment.

Those whose life has already been impacted and penetrated by God, his Word, and Will and they take heed and take to heart the proverbs will become wiser.

For those of us who have some understanding will receive guidance by studying, reading, meditating the meaning of the proverbs, teaching etc.

The foundation of TRUE Knowledge is the fear of the Lord.

Only fools will turn away from wisdom and discipline.

This scripture urges us to listen and accept correction from our earthly fathers as he listens to and receives corrections from Our Father in Heaven. Take heed to your mothers' instructions as she lives a God led life.

If your parents are living a life God led by God, then what you learn will bring you a level of grace and honor.

Hebrew 4:12 "God's Word is living and powerful. It is sharper than a sword that cuts both ways. It cuts straight into where the soul and spirit meet, and it divides them. It cuts into the joints and bones. It tells what the heart is thinking about and what it wants to do."

This scripture also establishes that the Word of God is knowledge.

BUT

It also is alive and full of the Word of God has the ability to invade or cut through.

The Word of God also can expose us; mind, body and soul.

Luke 11:28 " But He said, "Yes, but those who hear the Word of God and obey it are happy."

Jesus tells us that we are blessed to hear the Word of God and we are blessed to be able to do as the Word instructs.

Romans 8:7 "The mind that thinks only of ways to please the sinful old self is fighting against God. It is not able to obey God's Laws. It never can."

When our mind is not God centered and seeks to satisfy our flesh, our flesh is then not aligned with God. In this state our mind will not submit to God or his laws.

1 John 5:4 "Every child of God has power over the sins of the world. The way we have power over the sins of the world is by our faith."

All of us born of God were created to be overcomers of this world and Satan.

We are victorious and should walk in this victory daily which also leads to our increasing Faith.

John 16:13 "The Holy Spirit is coming. He will lead you into all truth. He will not speak His Own words. He will speak what He hears. He will tell you of things to come."

This scripture talks about what happens when the Holy Spirit come. We are guided buy God's Word when we are led by the Holy Spirit. The Holy Spirit isn't separate from God and can't operate without him but whatever God gives the Holy Spirit is shared and declare the things to come according to God and his Word.

2 Peter 1:2-3 "May you have more and more of His loving-favor and peace as you come to know God and our Lord Jesus Christ better. He gives us everything we need for life and for holy living. He gives it through His great power. As we come to know Him better, we learn that He called us to share His own shining-greatness and perfect life."

As we operate in the knowledge of God and Jesus, grace and peace will be multiplied upon us.

God's divine power blesses us with all things that pertains life and our walk and process as we become who od created us to be.

We shall experience his Glory and Excellence!

Luke 4:4 "Jesus said to him, "It is written, 'Man is not to live by bread alone.'"

Hallelujah!!! The Word of God is life and God's children need more than what feeds our physical body to live. The Word of God is NECESSARY.

1 Corinthians 12:8 "One person is given the gift of teaching words of wisdom. Another person is given the gift of teaching what he has learned and knows. These gifts are by the same Holy Spirit."

The Holy Spirit gives us the ability to give wise advice according to the Word of God which leads us both.

The Holy Spirits messages are of special knowledge.

John 3:16-17 "For God so loved the world that He gave His only Son. Whoever puts his trust in God's Son will not be lost but will have life that lasts forever. For God did not send His Son into the world to say it is guilty. He sent His Son so the world might be saved from the punishment of sin by Him."

Praise God for loving us, his children so much that he sacrificed his son Jesus so that we don't die, but have eternal life in the Kingdom of God.

Jesus was created and sent to save the world.

Hallelujah and for this we should all be grateful and should have a very clear understanding of our worth and value according to the Word of God and his plan for us all.

1 Corinthians 6:3 "Did you not know that we are to judge angels? So you should be able to take care of your problem here in this world without any trouble."

The Word of God should be used as the knowledge necessary to diffuse any situation and or disputes.

Feeding your Spirit man

Feeding your spirit man, is very important to your walk and process of becoming who God created you to be.

You must consistently feed your spirit man so that it is the strongest part of you and able to sustain your flesh when it is weak.

Your spirit man can stand for you when you can't.

Your Spirit man should be fed, trained, and used on a regular basis. Just like a muscle.

1 Peter 2:2-3 "As new babies want milk, you should want to drink the pure milk which is God's Word so you will grow up and be saved from the punishment of sin. If you have tasted of the Lord, you know how good He is."

Growth comes as we feed upon the infallible Word of God. Feeding your spirit man brings great nourishment that can be had no other way.

John 6:51 "I am the Living Bread that came down from heaven. If anyone eats this Bread, he will live forever. The Bread which I will give is My flesh. I will give this for the life of the world."

We must value our spirit man and the leading of that Spirit so that we are led by God, guided by the Holy Spirit, and fulfilling our purpose in the Kingdom of God.

Our flesh will fade, and our Spirit man will remain.

But we must de diligent in growing our Spirit man so that we can stand no matter what.

Your flesh will fail you, it wasn't designed to last, but your spirit man shall have eternal life.

Creating New Habits

As we evolve during this process of becoming who God created us to be, we must turn from those things that displease od and allow the new creature to become.

The new creature we become will be different, will intentionally create new habits, and ways of being according to the Word of God.

2 Corinthians 5:17-21 "For if a man belongs to Christ, he is a new person. The old life is gone. New life has begun. All this comes from God. He is the One Who brought us to Himself when we hated Him. He did this through Christ. Then He gave us the work of bringing others to Him. God was in Christ. He was working through Christ to bring the whole world back to Himself. God no longer held men's sins against them. And He gave us the work of telling and showing men this. We are Christ's missionaries. God is speaking to you through us. We are speaking for Christ and we ask you from our hearts to turn from your sins and come to God. Christ never sinned but God put our sin on Him. Then we are made right with God because of what Christ has done for us."

Isaiah 65:17-25 "For, see, I will make new heavens and a new earth. The past things will not be remembered or come to mind. But be glad and have joy forever in what I make. For see, I make Jerusalem for joy, and her people for happiness. I will have joy in Jerusalem and be glad in My people. The voice of crying will no longer be heard in it, or the cry of trouble. No more will there be in it a child who lives only a few days, or an old man who does not live many years. For the child will live to be a hundred years old. And the one who does not live a hundred years will be thought to be cursed. They will build houses and live in them. They will plant grapes and eat their fruit. They will not build a house and another live in it. They will not plant, and another eat. For My people will live a long time, like the days of a tree. And for a long time, my chosen ones will enjoy the work of their hands. They will not work for nothing or give birth to children and have trouble. For they will be the children of those who receive good from the Lord, and their children with them. And it will be before they call, I will answer. While they are still speaking, I will hear. The wolf and the lamb will eat together, and the lion will eat straw like the ox. And dust will be the snake's food. They will not hurt or destroy in all My holy mountain," says the Lord."

Revelation 21:1-8 "Then I saw a new heaven and a new earth. The first heaven and the first earth had passed away. There was no more sea. I saw the Holy City, the new Jerusalem. It was coming down out of heaven from God. It was made ready like a bride is made ready for her husband. I heard a loud voice coming from heaven. It said, "See! God's home is with men. He will live with them. They will be His people. God Himself will be with them. He will be their God. God will take away all their tears. There will be no more death or sorrow or crying or pain. All the old things have passed away." Then the One sitting on the throne said, "See! I am making all things new. Write, for these words are true and faithful." Then He said to me, "These things have happened! I am the First and the Last. I am the beginning and the end. To anyone who is thirsty, I will give the water of life. It is a free gift. He who has power and wins will receive these things. I will be his God and he will be My son. But those who are afraid and those who do not have faith and the sinful-minded people and those who kill other people and those who do sex sins and those who follow witchcraft and those who worship false gods and all those who tell lies will be put into the lake of fire and sulphur. This is the second death."

Matthew 9:16-17 "No one sews a piece of new cloth on an old coat, because if the new piece pulls away, it makes the hole bigger. Men do not put new wine into old skin bags. If they did, the skins would break and the wine would run out. The bags would be no good. They put new wine into new skin bags and both can be used."

Matthew 19:28-29 "Jesus said to them, "For sure, I tell you, when all the earth will be new and the Son of Man will sit on His throne in His shining-greatness, you who have followed Me will also sit on twelve thrones, and judge the twelve family groups of the Jewish nation. Everyone who has given up houses or brothers or sisters or father or mother or wife or children or lands because of Me, will get a hundred times more. And you will get life that lasts forever."

Galatians 2:20 "I have been put up on the cross to die with Christ. I no longer live. Christ lives in me. The life I now live in this body, I live by putting my trust in the Son of God. He was the One Who loved me and gave Himself for me."

Proverbs 3:5-6 "Trust in the Lord with all your heart, and do not trust in your own understanding. Agree with Him in all your ways, and He will make your paths straight. "

Colossians 3:9-10 "Do not lie to each other. You have put out of your life your old ways. You have now become a new person and are always learning more about Christ. You are being made more like Christ. He is the One Who made you."

Isaiah 43:18-19 "Do not remember the things that have happened before. Do not think about the things of the past. See, I will do a new thing. It will begin happening now. Will you not know about it? I will even make a road in the wilderness, and rivers in the desert."

Ezekiel 11:19-20 "I will give them one heart, and put a new spirit within them. I will take the heart of stone out of their flesh and give them a heart of flesh. Then they will walk in My Laws and keep them, and obey them. They will be My people, and I will be their God."

Ephesians 2:10 "We are His work. He has made us to belong to Christ Jesus so we can work for Him. He planned that we should do this."

2 Peter 1:4 "Through His shining-greatness and perfect life, He has given us promises. These promises are of great worth and no amount of money can buy them. Through these promises you can have God's own life in you now that you have gotten away from the sinful things of the world which came from wrong desires of the flesh."

Galatians 4:9-10 "But now that you know God, or should I say that you are known by God, why do you turn back again to the weak old Law? Why do you want to do those religious acts of worship that will keep you from being free? Why do you want to be held under the power of the Law again? You do special things on certain days and months and years and times of the year."

2 Corinthians 3:18 "All of us, with no covering on our faces, show the shining-greatness of the Lord as in a mirror. All the time we are being changed to look like Him, with more and more of His shining-greatness. This change is from the Lord Who is the Spirit."

1 Peter 3:18-22 "Christ suffered and died for sins once for all. He never sinned and yet He died for us who have sinned. He died so He might bring us to God. His body died but His spirit was made alive. Christ went and preached to the spirits in prison. Those were the spirits of the people who would not obey in the days of Noah. God waited a long time for them while Noah was building the big boat. But only eight people were saved from dying when the earth was covered with water. This is like baptism to us. Baptism does not mean we wash our bodies clean. It means we are saved from the punishment of sin and go to God in prayer with a heart that says we are right. This can be done because Christ was raised from the dead. Christ has gone to heaven and is on the right side of God. Angels and powers of heaven are obeying Him."

1 Titus 3:4-7 "But God, the One Who saves, showed how kind He was and how He loved us 5 by saving us from the punishment of sin. It was not because we worked to be right with God. It was because of His loving-kindness that He washed our sins away. At the same time He gave us new life when the Holy Spirit came into our lives. 6 God gave the Holy Spirit to fill our lives through Jesus Christ, the One Who saves. 7 Because of this, we are made right with God by His loving-favor. Now we can have life that lasts forever as He has promised."

2Corinthians 6:14-18 "Do not be joined together with those who do not belong to Christ. How can that which is good get along with that which is bad? How can light be in the same place with darkness? How can Christ get along with the devil? How can one who has put his trust in Christ get along with one who has not put his trust in Christ? How can the house of God get along with false gods? We are the house of the living God. God has said, "I will live in them and will walk among them. I will be their God and they will be My people. "The Lord has said, "So come out from among them. Do not be joined to them. Touch nothing that is sinful. And I will receive you. I will be a Father to you. You will be My sons and daughters, says the All-powerful God."

Romans 6:1-23 "What does this mean? Are we to keep on sinning so that God will give us more of His loving-favor? No, not at all! We are dead to sin. How then can we keep on living in sin? All of us were baptized to show we belong to Christ. We were baptized first of all to show His death. We were buried in baptism as Christ was buried in death. As Christ was raised from the dead by the great power of God, so we will have new life also. If we have become one with Christ in His death, we will be one with Him in being raised from the dead to new life. We know that our old life, our old sinful self, was nailed to the cross with Christ. And so the power of sin that held us was destroyed. Sin is no longer our boss. When a man is dead, he is free from the power of sin. And if we have died with Christ, we believe we will live with Him also. We know that Christ was raised from the dead. He will never die again. Death has no more power over Him. He died once but now lives. He died to break the power of sin, and the life He now lives is for God. You must do the same thing! Think of yourselves as dead to the power of sin. But now you have new life because of Jesus Christ our Lord. You are living this new life for God. So do not let sin have power over your body here on earth. You must not obey the body and let it do what it wants to do. Do not give any part of your body for sinful use. Instead, give yourself to God as a living person who has been raised from the dead. Give every part of your body to God to do what is right. Sin must not have power over you. You are not living by the Law. You have life because of God's loving-favor. What are we to do then? Are we to sin because we have God's loving-favor and are not living by the Law? No, not at all! Do you not know that when you give yourself as a servant to be owned by someone, that one becomes your owner? If you give yourself to sin, the end is death. If you give yourself to God, the end is being right with Him. At one time you were held by the power of sin. But now you obey with all your heart the teaching that was given to you. Thank God for this! You were made free from the power of sin. Being right with God has power over you now. I speak with words easy to understand because your human thinking is weak. At one time you gave yourselves over to the power of sin. You kept on sinning all the more. Now give yourselves over to being right with God. Set yourself apart for God-like living and to do His work. When sin had power over your life, you were not right with God. What good did you get from the things you are ashamed of now? Those things bring death. But now you are free from the power of sin. You have become a servant for God. Your life is set apart for God-like living. The end is life that lasts forever. You get what is coming to you when you sin. It is death! But God's free gift is life that lasts forever. It is given to us by our Lord Jesus Christ."

Step into the fullness of who od created you to be expecting to receive and d according to God's Word, Plan, and Purpose.

The foundation scriptures provided shows you what God expects from and for us and what he promises us.

Obedience is the key that unlocks the blessings. Faith is the key that releases the promises.

Turn from your old ways, change and allow the Holy Spirit to lead you in becoming who God created you to be!

You are not your past and your past can't and won't dictate your future which is in God's hands.

Remember who created you!

You are loved and valued as God's creations; a masterpiece created by the Great I am!

Its Easier to be who God created you to be!

Often we complicate our life by trying to be someone or something we are not and not even created to be.

You were created unique in all ways, created to do something only you can be and do!

The more you work on becoming who od created you to be the easier life will get.

Key things I will urge you to do:

1. Seek God 1st in all things, and if you can't seek him about it, it is probably wrong and should not be entertaining the thought anyway.

2. Seek to ONLY please God in your walk. Pleasing God will manifest a trickle down effect and any and everyone who is expected to be impacted by you will be positively affected by your choice to please God, obey his Word, and follow the leading of the Holy Spirit.

3. Recognize that od is always doing 1 of 3 things in our life:

   a. Pruning

   b. Preserving

   c. Preparing

   God isn't wasteful!!

4. Want what God wants for you. He knows best.

5. Don't just do it because you can, wait on the Lord, and the leading of the Holy Spirit.

6. Don't spend your lifetime, energy, on trying to be someone else. You can't manifest someone else's destiny in your life.

7. Focus on your strength and weaknesses

8. Celebrate the things about you that are unique.

God's plan for you is just as awesome!

Your future is just as bright!

Chapter 9
The Journey: The Real Reality; Seeing things God's does

How does God see this world?

Samuel 16:7 "But the Lord said to Samuel, "Do not consider his appearance or his height, for I have rejected him. The Lord does not look at the things people look at. People look at the outward appearance, but the Lord looks at the heart."

The Lord is both clear and consistent on these instructions which contradict how the world tries to appeal to us. The world tells us to do just the opposite. And it is this thing that comes against and speak against God, his Word that we should always reject and don't allow the thoughts or concept to become a part of your thought process.

God looks from the inside out for he knows the outside is tainted, and deceiving.

It is when we allow who we are on the inside to overflow to our outside that one can trust what they see.

We should all look at each other heart.

This goes back to the saying "never judge a book by its cover." The inside is where our truth lives or hides depending on the person.

Psalm 119:18 "Open my eyes to see the wonderful truths in your instructions."

In this scripture we yearn for hi instructions as it leads to all truths; God's truths are wonderful and eye opening.

1 John 4:1 "Beloved, do not believe every spirit; instead test the spirits to see whether they are from God, because many false prophets and teachers have gone out into the world.

God is always concerned about us being misled especially by people who claim to represent him. Any representative of God will be easily recognized as we test them, their actions, words, and behaviors against the Word of God.

The Word of God is infallible.

These people aren't doing it for God or his Glory which is another clear sign.

Don't be scared to challenge those who come and don't be deceived by their fake good deeds, and misleading words and truth.

God's Word stands alone.

Isaiah 41:10 "Don't be afraid, for I am with you. Don't be discouraged, for I am your God. I will strengthen you and help you. I will hold you up with my victorious right hand."

Hallelujah this is some good word. Word you can believe in and stand on confidently knowing God is not a man that, can't and won't lie. His Word is true! It is the light that leads to all understanding.

Don't fear your future when your steps have been ordered!

Don't fear when God is in control, he has your best interest at heart and there is no failure in his plan.

Promises to strengthen us and help us. We mess up here because we try to draw from another's strength when God promises us his. We often times seek help from those we assume can help. God is intentional with all connections and relationships. He sends the help or leads us to our help. Stay in Gods Will, there is guarantee there you can get no where else. God is always looking out for us.

Job 34:21 "For God watches how people live; he sees everything they do."

Our Father in Heaven, is all knowing. He takes a real interest in how we live. He isn't blind to anything we do, the good, bad, and the ugly.

We can't hide what we do or why we do it. So make sure your heart, motives, and intent are aligned with God's Word.

Isaiah 6:10 "Harden the hearts of these people. Plug their ears and shut their eyes. That way, they will not see with their eyes, nor hear with their ears, nor understand with their hearts and turn to me for healing."

This is something we often experience in our process of becoming who God created us to be. At some point you will come to point where anything you depend on or count on will fail you or be unavailable for a variety of reasons.

But it is these times where there is no where to go but to God. Depend on your creator who says he has you and looking out for you.

Your flesh and other people will fail you because its human nature.

God never tells us to trust people or trust our flesh, but he does tell us to seek him, and trust who he send on his behalf.

God wants us to depend solely on Him, His Word for guidance and the Holy Spirit for instructions on how to become who we were created to be.

Turn to Him!

Make Him your focus!

Make his plan, Your Plan!

Make your purpose a Priority!

Embrace your process as it is necessary in your journey.

Hebrews 4:12-13 "For the word of God is alive and powerful. It is sharper than the sharpest two-edged sword, cutting between soul and spirit, between joint and marrow. It exposes our innermost thoughts and desires. Nothing in all creation is hidden from God. Everything is naked and exposed before his eyes, and he is the one to whom we are accountable."

The Word of God is alive and powerful and necessary as a guide for living a life acceptable and pleasing to God.

As we live and act on the Word our inner thoughts and desires are exposed.

God sees all and knows all and it would behoove you to be mindful of this concept, and act, do, and behave accordingly.

Its your choice to choose and its up to you to act on the knowledge God has given us.

Man accountable to man is not accountable at all.

Man accountable to God is true accountability.

Ephesians 4:2-3 "Always be humble and gentle. Be patient with each other, making allowance for each other's faults because of your love. Make every effort to keep yourselves united in the Spirit, binding yourselves together with peace."

God uses certain verbiage that tells the frequency in which he expects us to do things.

For example God wants us to <u>Always</u> be humble and gentle. Not sometimes, not when things are good, not when you need something or someone, BUT ALWAYS.

Being humble allows you to be compassionate to others who are walking their walk and progressing through to their purpose.

Understand that God doesn't expect perfection and it is in our imperfections is where he can show up and perfect things about and within us.

We learn from mistakes!

We grow from failed attempts!

Learn>Grow>Embrace>Progress>Purpose>Destiny>The Kingdom of God

We can help others by walking our walk, let others see God in you, your life, and process.

Sign up and Sell out!

You

Your life

Your Future

They are all worth it!

One Body   >   Many Parts

One Kingdom   >   Many Roles

Remain spirit led and unite in peace!

Amos 3:7 "Surely the Lord GOD does nothing without revealing His secret plan of the judgment to come
To His servants the prophets."

God hides nothings, send people, signs, His Word and the Holy Spirit to reveal his plans. It is never a guessing game.

Pray for clarity, and God will make it plain.

Proverbs 15:3 "The eyes of the Lord are in every place, watching the evil and the good."

God is all knowing, he hears all and he sees all. Watches everyone, believer and non-believers.

Ephesians 5:18 "Don't be drunk with wine because that will ruin your life. Instead, be filled with the Holy Spirit.

Anything done in excess, serving only your flesh and having no spiritual benefit should not be done at all.

Never do anything that only serves the flesh. Be filled and led by the Holy Spirit and be forever changed with greater connection to our Heavenly Father.

Luke 6:42 "How can you think of saying, 'Friend, let me help you get rid of that speck in your eye,' when you can't see past the log in your own eye? Hypocrite! First get rid of the log in your own eye; then you will see well enough to deal with the speck in your friend's eye."

This scripture normally causes one to say ouch because at some point we have all been guilty.

You cannot help someone if you need help. You can't tell someone how to get right when you living wrong.

God showed me years ago that I could do more good by walking my own path than trying to help someone walk their own.

We need to see how it is done, because it is our process to go through.

Be a person of action; follow your own good advice, so others can see just how good it really is.

I always say, you can't help me go where I'm going if you have never been.

1 Timothy 1:7 "For God has not given us a spirit of fear and timidity, but of power, love, and self-discipline."

God has given us so much and praise him right now, for what he did not give us.

No Fear!

No being timid!

Be bold, confident, and courageous!

Because of God, we are full of power!

God loves us unconditionally, and for this we should be grateful, sense we all long for love.

God is love!

Self-discipline and Self-control

> ➢ Self-discipline is the process of us controlling ourselves based on the rules, regulations based on God's Word.

Obedience to the Word of God lead to self-discipline.

> ➢ Self-control is the process of controlling all aspects of life believing you can alter or determine the outcome.

God's Word helps us and led us to a disciplined life.

Luke 4:18-19 "The Spirit of the LORD is upon me, for he has anointed me to bring Good News to the poor. He has sent me to proclaim that captives will be released, that the blind will see, that the oppressed will be set free, and that the time of the LORD's favor has come."

When we receive the Holy Spirit and choose to live a Holy Spirit Lead life, we will be anointed.

Anointed for the benefit of the kingdom to bring God's good and infallible Word to the Poor, to encourage and remind them of who God is and his promises.

God will amount us to help free others who are being held captive by their poor choices and the devils deception and misguidance.

The spirit of God can help free the oppressed and help the blind see, by anointing willing believers.

Let the Lord use you!

Be a willing vessel!

1 Corinthian 4:5 "So don't make judgments about anyone ahead of time—before the Lord returns. For he will bring our darkest secrets to light and will reveal our private motives. Then God will give to each one whatever praise is due."

Stay in your zone, your lane, mind your own yard.

Judge no one because you don't know their path or journey, they have traveled or the one God has planned for them.

When the Jesus Lord returns our darkest secrets to light and will reveal our private motives.

Everyone will be rewarded accordingly.

Isaiah 5:21 "What sorrow for those who are wise in their own eyes and think themselves so clever."

God is sadden by those that consider themselves smart or wise because of knowledge that is not Godly or did it come from God.

The Word of God makes us wise.

1 Chronicles 16:11 "Search for the LORD and for his strength; continually seek him."

Seek God in all things and at all times about all things.

This will keep you, your life, your choices, and your future aligned with God's Word, God's Will, and God's ways.

These is protection and certainty when we seek and follow!

Romans 10:9 "If you openly declare that Jesus is Lord and believe in your heart that God raised him from the dead, you will be saved."

This scripture is very specific about what it takes to be saved.

It begins with us confessing what we believe in our heart, body, and mind. How we act on this belief leads to us being saved.

Zephaniah 3:17 "For the LORD your God is living among you. He is a mighty savior. He will take delight in you with gladness. With his love, he will calm all your fears. He will rejoice over you with joyful songs."

This scripture reminds us that God is always with us guiding and watching.

He finds pleasure in our happiness.

He gives us his unconditional love to conquer our fears.

Hebrews 1:3 "The Son radiates God's own glory and expresses the very character of God, and he sustains everything by the mighty power of his command. When he had cleansed us from our sins, he sat down in the place of honor at the right hand of the majestic God in heaven.

As children of God, we are to radiate God's Glory and be visible images and expressions of who God is and what he stands for. Everything for us is sustained by the mighty power of his command.

Be grateful for Jesus, the son of God cleansed us from our sins.

What a sacrifice and gift.

Ephesians 1:4 "Even before he made the world, God loves us and chose us in Christ to be holy and without fault in his eyes."

God's love is a priceless gift that he gave and chose us to receive as well as being Holy and having no fault.

I love the way God sees us.

No pressure, such freedom in the things of God.

Galatians 2:20 "My old self has been crucified with Christ. It is no longer I who live, but Christ lives in me. So I live in this earthly body by trusting in the Son of God, who loved me and gave himself for me."

This is in reference to every believer. Our old self is no longer and we shouldn't take part in things that are familiar and comfortable to your old self.

John 3:16-17 "For this is how God loved the world: He gave his one and only Son, so that everyone who believes in him will not perish but have eternal life. God sent his Son into the world not to judge the world, but to save the world through him."

God sacrificed his Son so that we may have life, eternal life, and a life of abundance, free of sickness, and free of lack.

Because of Jesus we are saved.

John 1:11-14 "He came to his own people, and even they rejected him. But to all who believed him and accepted him, he gave the right to become children of God. They are reborn—not with a physical birth resulting from human passion or plan, but a birth that comes from God. So the

Word became human and made his home among us. He was full of unfailing love and faithfulness. And we have seen his glory, the glory of the Father's one and only Son."

Believing God leads us ti accepting God, His Will, and Word.

This rebirth is not physical, it is supernatural, spiritual and from God.

This rebirth activated the Word, which allowed it to take human form, now the Word is alive. Word of God is now human.

This form carries with it unfailing love and faithfulness.

Because of our beliefs, we will get to see his Glory!

Proverbs 20:12 "Ears to hear and eyes to see both are gifts from the LORD."

This scripture refers to both the physical and scripture eyes and ears.

Physical eyes and ears are used in the natural realm.

Spiritual eyes and ears are used in the supernatural realm.

1 JOHN 1:9 "But if we confess our sins to him, he is faithful and just to forgive us our sins and to cleanse us from all wickedness."

No one is perfect, we are all sinners, and we all fall short.

Do not lie to yourself, lying to yourself makes it easier for you to accept the lies of other.

God tells us when we win we must confess and turn from those things.

Praise God for his faithfulness, and because of his grace and mercy, he forgives us and cleanse us.

2 Corinthians 4:4 "Satan, who is the god of this world, has blinded the minds of those who don't believe. They are unable to see the glorious light of the Good News. They don't understand this message about the glory of Christ, who is the exact likeness of God."

Satan is the god of this world, and as we covered in chapter 6 he is the king of lies and deception. One of his most successful tactics is blinding the mind preventing it from seeing the truth.

John 16:33 "I have told you all this so that you may have peace in me. Here on earth you will have many trials and sorrows. But take heart, because I have overcome the world."

Praise God, we are overcomers of this world. God wants us to have peace in him, in his way, we will obtain peace, in him word we receive peace.

God warns us that there will be trials, tribulations, and sorrow further signifying that there is no perfect life to be had.

But believe in what God says because of Him, His Word, His Ways, and His Will. We are victorious and are overcomers of things of this world.

2 Timothy 3:16 "All Scripture is inspired by God and is useful to teach us what is true and to make us realize what is wrong in our lives. It corrects us when we are wrong and teaches us to do what is right."

The Word of God is the most important and useful information we can receive to help us learn what is true so that we may live according to God's Holy Word.

The bible teaches us right from wrong, we just have to learn and obey.

Colossian 1:15-16 "Christ is the visible image of the invisible God. He existed before anything was created and is supreme over all creation, for through him God created everything in the heavenly realms and on earth.
He made the things we can see and the things we can't see—such as thrones, kingdoms, rulers, and authorities in the unseen world. Everything was created through him and for him."

The Son of God was born with purpose, he serves as the visible representation of who God our Father is.

God existed before anything

Christ is supreme over all things

God is a master creator, creating everything in the heavenly realm and here on Earth.

Acts 2:38 "Peter replied, "Each of you must repent of your sins and turn to God, and be baptized in the name of Jesus Christ for the forgiveness of your sins. Then you will receive the gift of the Holy Spirit.

This Word is specific and direct and should be taken at face value. God instructs us throughout the bible to repent and turn from the people and things that are not of God which lead to the forgiveness of our sins.

After these come to pass you can then receive one of God's greatest gifts.... The Holy Spirit!

1 Corinthians 6:19-20 "Don't you realize that your body is the temple of the Holy Spirit, who lives in you and was given to you by God? You do not belong to yourself, for God bought you with a high price. So you must honor God with your body."

God reminds us through this scripture that our body and flesh houses our spirit man.

God wants us to take care of our body so that it will last through our process as we become who God created you to be.

Your body belongs to God so you must honor God completely... Mind, Body, and Soul.

1 Chronicles 16:9 "Sing to him; yes, sing his praises. Tell everyone about his wonderful deeds."

Glorify God for who he is, and all he does. Testify as a witness of his great deeds, so others will know God is real and alive and working in all of our lives.

Exodus 15:2 "The lord is my strength and my son;he has given me victory."

Hallelujah, we have the victory right now in Jesus Name!

Our Father is our strength and he gives my heart a song for which honors, praises, and glorifies God as the head of our lives.

Our Real Reality – In the Supernatural

The supernatural realm is where God operates on a higher level, where his Word is true, alive, and working.

The supernatural is where we receive according to the Word, Plan, and Purpose of our lives.

In this realm, we experience miracles, and the unexplainable.

The devil has no place in this realm and is completely powerless.

We can't be touched in this realm.

There is protection and guarantees in the spiritual realm.

When in the supernatural realm our discernment is at an all time high and we see the devil coming and are very aware of all of his attempts to kill, steal, and destroy us.

In the supernatural realm is where you experience the life God planned for you.

Obedience in this realm lead to great rewards and success like no other.

The supernatural realm is where you can live freely following God's rules and the leading of the Holy Spirit.

In this realm you may tend to experience supernatural blessing, favor, and power.

In this realm there is a greater connection to our creator.

Choose to reside in the supernatural, so your steps will be ordered and protected.

Choose the supernatural realm so that you and your future is going according to God's plan and his Will for our life.

Separate yourself from the natural.

Romans 12:2 "And do not be conformed to this world but be transformed and progressively changed by the renewing of your mind, so that you may prove what the will of God is, that which is good and acceptable and perfect."

Make the supernatural realm your place of protection, comfort, and guarantees based on God's Word, plan, purpose, and will.

The supernatural realm is where we thrive, grow, and nature spiritually.

Truth of the Matter

Good or Bad it will workout for our good if we love the Lord, obey his commands and follow the leading of the Holy Spirit.

We must tap into our creator to ensure our lives are aligned with God's Will for each of us.

Don't go through life personalizing the decisions of others just because your life is somehow affected. God is never surprised and always steps ahead.

We live out God's past!

Its already done; we are just waiting for the appointed time and appointed place for the things of God to happen.

God has the solution before the problem even arises.

It is our choices and inability to trust God that causes us to go through things that weren't apart of God's original plan for your life.

We refuse to see ourselves as he does, which prevents us from doing the thing we were created and purposed to do.

We refuse to think like God, so we cant move, act, or receive according to his plan, will, and word.

We refuse to believe in God with all our hearts, preventing us from experiencing this world and life the way God planned for us.

Truth of the matter is od's word which is true will make all the difference in your life, your family and future.

The Word of God is true and it leads us in the way we should go and ANYTHING that contradicts must be ignored and disregarded. Avoid any and all distractions from Satan.

You are to use the Word of God to know, understand, and believe so that you can become all God created you to be....

AND

Do all he created you to do

Achieve every goal he set for you to achieve.

Allow your life to be a living testimony of who God is!

Tell the Truth

Live By the Truth

The Word of God is infallible!

Don't get Distracted

Distraction comes in many forms.

Visual

Financial

Family

Personal Desires(That serve the flesh)

Distractions were created to throw us off course and to make us see things in a way that would cause us to take our eyes off God and his plan.

We must desire God's plan for our life above our own, the world, or our family.

Simplify your life

Seek God in all things so you will know in your Spirit what is of God and what is not.

Pray daily for discernment, which will cause you to be distraction high alert.

The good thing about a distraction is that it is temporary and because God's goodness our paths are always available to get back on.

God is a God of many chances.

Stay focused on the Word of God as your primary focus.

Obey his Word no matter what.

Have the ultimate follow through. Don't stop till you achieve what God created you to achieve.

Receiving according to God's Word is the ultimate reward that will cause other believers and non-believers to know and receive from God for themselves.

Your Journey Belongs to you

Along this journey we will be called to play roles in the lives of others, but this is only one part of who we are.

And just as you should not personalize the decisions of others; don't personalize your decision based on the lives of others.

Being a mother, father, sister, brother, grandparent are only aspects of who we are.

The only role or title that can and will dictate who we are, what we do, what we become, what we receive is being a "child of God."

On this journey simplify your life and seek to:

Only please God

Only follow God

Only listen to God

Only obey God

If you do these things you will be free to live and choose better decisions based on God's truth and his plan for your life.

Choose God above all others

Follow God above all others

Believe in God above all others

Let God be God

Know that he is all knowing and all powerful.

He always has your best interest at heart and the Kingdom of God in mind.

Don't stay bound to the things God chose to free you of.

Don't see to receive from others what God promises you.

Accept God for who he is; allow him to show up for you.

Elohim – Refers to God's incredible power and might

The One and Only God

The Supreme Being > The creator

El Shaddai – God the Almighty

Jehovah – God the Lord

Jehovah Raah – Lord my Shepherd

Jireh – Lord that sees and provides

Rapha – Healer and Restorer

Tsidkenu – Lord of Righteousness

Shalom – Lord of Peace

Shammah – Lord is present with me

Nissi – Lord is my protection and covering

Let God be who he promises to be for you.

Be a willing vessel to be led, taught, used for a greater purpose.

Want to be a part of something bigger than yourself.

Accept your uniqueness, greatness, and purpose

And enjoy the rest of your life as you embrace God, his plan, purpose, Word, and Will.

This is your life

Your journey

Your Process

Embrace it and accept all that is yours according to the mighty Word of God.

Be Humble and Let God be God!

Made in the USA
Columbia, SC
03 April 2021